A Little Girl in Auschwitz

Lidia Maksymowicz has shared her story in the Auschwitz museum, which she visits every year. It was also the focus of a documentary by the Italian association 'La Memoria Viva'.

Paolo Rodari was the first journalist to interview Lidia Maksymowicz in Rome. He is a Vatican correspondent for the Italian newspaper *la Repubblica* and the author of several bestselling books.

LIDIA MAKSYMOWICZ

with Paolo Rodari

A Little Girl in Auschwitz

A heart-wrenching true story of survival, hope and love

Translated by Shaun Whiteside

PAN BOOKS

First published 2022 by RCS MediaGroup S.p.A., Milano

First published in the UK 2023 by Macmillan

This paperback edition published 2024 by Pan Books
an imprint of Pan Macmillan
The Smithson, 6 Briset Street, London EC1M 5NR
EU representative: Macmillan Publishers Ireland Ltd, 1st Floor,
The Liffey Trust Centre, 117–126 Sheriff Street Upper,
Dublin 1, D01 YC43
Associated companies throughout the world
www.panmacmillan.com

ISBN 978-1-5290-9440-4

5 7 9 8 6 4

A CIP catalogue record for this book is available from the British Library.

Plate section courtesy of Lidia Skibicka Maksymowicz / La Memoria Viva association
in Castellamonte (TO)

Typeset by Palimpsest Book Production, Falkirk, Stirlingshire
Printed and bound by CPI Group (UK) Ltd, Croydon, CR0 4YY

MIX
Paper | Supporting
responsible forestry
FSC
www.fsc.org
FSC® C116313

Visit **www.panmacmillan.com** to read more about all our books
and to buy them. You will also find features, author interviews and
news of any author events, and you can sign up for e-newsletters
so that you're always first to hear about our new releases.

This book is dedicated to the children who didn't have the good fortune to survive the hell of Birkenau, and to my two mothers, to whom I owe my life.

Contents

Introduction by Pope Francis

I am happy that the book by Lidia, survivor of Auschwitz-Birkenau extermination camp, is coming out on International Day of Commemoration. The hope is that this work will help us to remember what happened. Remembering is indeed an expression of humanity; remembering is a sign of civilization; remembering is the condition for a better future of peace and brotherhood. The words I said at the General Audience on 28 January 2021 still apply today: 'Remembering is being careful because these things could happen again, beginning with ideological proposals intended to save a people and ending by destroying a people and humanity: we must be attentive to how this path of death, of extermination and brutality began.'

When, on 26 May 2021, I briefly greeted Lidia in the San Damaso Courtyard, I wanted to kiss the arm tattooed with the number imposed upon her in Auschwitz-Birkenau: 70072. It was a simple gesture of reconciliation, so that the memory of the past may be kept alive, and so that we may learn from the dark pages of history so as not to repeat it, so as never to make the same mistakes again. So we go on trying tirelessly to cultivate justice, to increase harmony and maintain integration, to be instruments of peace and builders of a better world. In this way we advance the mission of Lidia, who said a year ago that 'the mission I have chosen and which I will take forward for as long as I live and remember is to talk about what happened to me'. And again: 'To tell it above all to the young, so that they never allow such a thing to happen again.'

Message from Liliana Segre,
Holocaust survivor

Lidia's story is a fragment of the concentration-camp universe; the damned place is Birkenau; the events related are a game of dice with death. It is set against the most unspeakable background of the tragedies of the twentieth century. This is Year Zero of civilization.

Why are we still talking about it? Out of duty: the duty of memory. Now and always, like a mantra of the third millennium. The key word is memory, that special category which, if used well, allows us to keep democracy in good health. Those who forget, on the other hand, are more exposed to the dangers of violence and intolerance.

But how do we vaccinate ourselves against the 'virus of hate'?

By studying history and applying the constitution from which everything derives.

I wish the boys and girls who browse these pages a good

future, free from the shadow of the past – a time that doesn't pass for someone like me, who still feels a little bit drowned and a little bit saved.

Message from Sami Modiano, Holocaust survivor

I was very moved to meet someone like Lidia, and couldn't help hugging her!

Her story is like my own – one of loneliness and the terrible experience of those extermination camps, torn from her mother's hands at only three years old, facing the uncertainty of what was to come.

So many things bring us together in the painful experience of our past, but the desire not to surrender to it has helped us to overcome the obstacles of life.

The wound remains, but just as Lidia found her mother after many years and told her dramatic story, I too found a person who looked after me and who has always been close to me: my wife Selma. Lidia's book must remain as an example of life: strength, courage, perseverance in goodness, love of one's neighbour and no more wars!

After being silent for so many years, like her I too have decided to speak, to externalize my experience and to leave my message: 'Never again.'

1

JUST A FEW FLASHES. LIKE LIGHTNING BOLTS in the darkness of a night far off in time and yet as close as if it were yesterday. They have accompanied me for decades, since I was deported with my mother to the extermination camp.

I'm almost four. She is twenty-two.

She is holding me in her arms when we leave the train at Birkenau. It is December 1943. It is freezing cold. The snow falls like ice. The wind whips us. Desolation all around us. I look at the reddish-brown carriage in which we have travelled crammed together for days, our legs numb, with the feeling that we could die at any moment. There is a powerful temptation to board the train again. A moment ago, all I wanted was to get off the train, to get some oxygen and air. Now I don't; I want to get back on board. Go back. Go home.

I remember a tight embrace. My mother covering my face. Or perhaps I'm trying to plunge my face into her chest, already much thinner after a journey that seemed endless. The train constantly sped up and slowed down. Long stops in unfamiliar landscapes.

Some German soldiers divide the new arrivals into two rows. A few dozen yards behind us, others are keeping watch from the top of a brick tower. We end up in the row on the right. Many go to the left, however, chosen from the oldest, probably the ones who are considered the frailest and weakest. There are few clues as to how it will end up. There are no words; only resignation. They lack the energy to revolt in any way. There isn't enough strength to make any kind of rebellion effective.

I smell bad, and so does my mother. And so does everyone who has just got off the train. And yet that smell is the only friendly, familiar thing in an alien world. Where have we ended up? No one speaks; no one offers any explanations. We are here and that's that.

The barking of the dogs is something I have never forgotten. Even today, when a dog barks in the street, my mind goes back there, to that pier suspended between snow and wind as the soldiers shout in an unknown language. Often the SS men – I will learn that that's what they're called – return to me in sleep, in dreams that seem real. And which wake me up suddenly in the depths of the night, sweating, terrified, trembling. They shout and I don't understand the meaning of their words. Then there's the spitting, contemptuous laughter, eyes filled with hate.

The animals are kept on leads. They foam at the mouth, held back by the whips of the Germans. They enjoy pushing them towards us and the dogs bare their teeth, rise up on their back legs without realizing that the prey they have in front of them have already surrendered. They are already dead.

My mother is brutally separated from me, like other mothers from other children. Cries and weeping. She is taken away, I don't know where. I see her again shortly afterwards, shaven and completely naked. She hasn't a single hair on her head. This must be when I, too, have my head shaved, my own clothes taken away and replaced. I don't remember this happening; I just remember how my mother hugs me. And smiles. I remember, she smiles at me as if to say: don't worry, everything's fine. I ask her: *where did your braids go?* She doesn't reply. *And Grandpa and Grandma? Where did they go?* She still doesn't answer.

We look towards the back of the camp. Black smoke comes from two chimneys. I will find out in due course that they are the outlets for the flames in the ovens of the crematoria. Soot that covers the sky. Soot which, they will tell me, clogs the lungs of the Polish citizens who live in the nearby area, beyond Oświęcim, beyond the Vistula. The stench of burnt meat. The smell of death. We don't say anything. No one says anything. The Poles breathe it in too, unable to react. We can only guess at what's happening. I understand something bad has happened to my grandparents.

Beyond the chimneys there's barbed wire. Beyond the barbed wire, bare trees. A plain that disappears into the unknown. I wish I could be out there; I wish I could run towards freedom, far, as far as possible. Freedom is so close, and yet at the same time so unattainable. I'm told that some people tried to climb the wire. And they were electrocuted. Others were machine-gunned just before they could escape.

Today I try to reconstruct all the things that happened to me. At the age of over eighty I can't say whether the flashes that appear in my memory like sharpened blades are the product of my real experiences or what friends who survived, a few years older than me, have told me, years later, that they went through along with me. The only certainty is that I was there; I have been there. My memories and the stories told by other people are superimposed upon one another until they become jumbled up together. And I can no longer fully distinguish what is mine and what is theirs. But there's nothing I can do about it. And so it goes.

When I entered the camp I was very young. When I left I was already four years old, turning five. I was one of the children who spent the longest time in there, perhaps one of the youngest ones who managed to survive, to save herself. Sometimes I can't help wondering: was I too young to be able to tell my story today? Hard to say. What is certain is that thirteen months in Birkenau will leave deep marks whatever your age. Those days, months, years are a wound that has always gone with me and which will, I know, go with me until the end of my days. And the fact that I don't remember everything in perfect order only intensifies the pain of that wound. I am not fully aware of all the abuses to which I was subjected. And yet they existed. And yet they exist. They live inside me, in my subconscious. They are my travelling companions. Unwieldy and present at the same time. They influence my days. My silences. My smiles followed by moments of sadness. Birkenau never dies. Birkenau is an indelible part of what I have been through. It is a monster that goes on talking, communicating its unspeakable experience.

I realize this in retrospect, after every meeting in which I am called upon to bear witness, to travel the world telling the story of what I have been through. Every time I find myself saying something I hadn't said before. Details buried in my mind return to the surface and find new words that surprise me first of all, then my family members and those who love me: you've never told me that before. I know, I reply. It's always been inside me but only now has it found a way to come out. I really think that it's because I was a child in Birkenau. Children store things up, sometimes they hide them, at other times they get confused, but they don't forget, ever. And when they grow up they relive what happened to them with new kinds of awareness. What the mind buries does not die. It comes back to life. It returns to life over time. And often it achieves full awareness of what happened only after years, decades even. That's how it is for many people. And that's how it is for me.

What was done to me in those long months in prison? My body experienced things, my mind stored them up and then it also buried them. And still, year after year, it has released them, as the sea gives up its wreckage.

I often think of my spirit. I compare it to an ancient

glacier melting. In Birkenau, the freezing cold covered everything: emotions, feelings, words. And then, slowly, the ice made way for different seasons. The temperature outside gradually became milder. And what was once covered over is now coming back to light.

Having to come to terms with all this is far from easy. It is my life's task. Arduous but also indispensable. I do it for myself, of course. But I also do it for everyone else, for my friends and acquaintances, for my friends' friends, for people I don't know but who are part of the same human family as I am. I want to be clear, I want to set out as completely as I can what I think: the darkness of the camps is not archived once and for all. The hatred that fed those places is always lying in wait; it can re-emerge at any time. One has to be particularly careful with memory, with the story of what has been. What was the point of the winters in the extermination camps? What if not at least to ensure that humanity might become aware of its darkest side and to do its very best to avoid the same thing rising up again, having a voice, having citizenship, energy, a life force? What is the point of Birkenau, and what is the point of all the extermination camps if not to ensure that darkness does not envelop us again?

I read in the papers about new kinds of anti-Semitism. For those who, like me, experienced the camps, it seems impossible and yet vital. Because for us survivors of the camps they are not events of decades ago; they are things that happened yesterday, a few hours ago; they are infernos from which we have just escaped. They are here, around the corner, and we have just managed to dodge them, to change direction. So it's always possible to fall back into them.

What was the mistake that was made before the camps opened? Giving citizenship to words of hostility that were beyond all logic, but that were suddenly granted legitimacy. It's still like that today. We are beginning to allow words that bear the whiff of hatred, division, exclusion. When I hear them in the mouths of politicians I find I can't breathe. Here, in my Europe, in my home, those terrible words. It's right now, at moments like this, that the darkness can fall upon me again. We will never forget it.

My mother was a very beautiful woman. On the train to hell she had long fair hair in braids. She was strong, athletic and proud of her origins. Belarussian, a descendant of the Slavic tribes of the East. A partisan, resisting all invaders, she capitulated only when she was captured by the Nazis late in 1943. But in the camp she went on fighting; she went on resisting. In Birkenau her strategy was one of silence. In the forests of Belorussia, she talked, she issued orders, she organized the defence of our people. She was an active presence. In Birkenau, on the other hand, she did the opposite. She stopped talking. She faked indifference towards the enemy. And most of all she learned to creep.

From her barrack to mine – I have realized recently when I have gone back to visit that place of death – there was a distance of only about fifty metres. There was a third barrack in between. She risked it from time to time. And she came to find me. Posted on a wooden tower was a German clutching a rifle. He observed every movement and anyone who made a mistake would come to a bad end. If he saw her creeping, it would be the end: a shooting squad or the gas chamber were inevitable. But she came out anyway. She plunged into the darkness. She hid among the grass and mud. She crept. Fearlessly, she crept.

What I remember above all about our meetings are the hugs. There was no food. And yet every now and again she managed to bring me onions. I ate them a little bit at a time, first put in my mouth by her emaciated fingers, then all alone in the darkness of night. Sometimes between my teeth I would find dirt, soil. There was no water to clean the onions. They were eaten just as they are, not wasting the tiniest bit. I didn't share them with anyone. One instinct guided me above all: the instinct to survive. Perhaps it's a terrible thing to admit, but that's how things were. And the same was true of the other children. It was an animal instinct, fierce and brutal. That was what we had become. It was what we were. In Birkenau, it's what united us.

I admit that I struggle to remember much of what we said to one another. There must have been conversations. But of those I remember only a few phrases, among them one that I said to her and which goes more or less like this: *please don't just leave me onions; leave me your hands too, to keep me company in the dark.*

The nights in the camp were terrible: the terror of the darkness, the sense of being abandoned, of being lost for ever.

My mother's hands were dirty, gaunt. They clutched at tufts of grass as she crept through the darkness. Sometimes they groped in the mud – her black nails in the rain-drenched earth, feeling their way, a few feet at a time.

When she was sure she hadn't been seen, she would steal from her own barrack to the children's barrack, mine,

18

the one reserved for the guinea pigs of Dr Josef Mengele. She searched for me among the wooden tiers that served as beds. Each bunk had three, placed one above the other along the rectangular perimeter of the barrack. And in there we too were on top of one another, crammed together like ants. I learned early on that it was better to be in the top bunk, the one closest to the ceiling, where the filth of your companions was less likely to fall on you. Still, I didn't always manage to get that one, and sometimes I had to settle for being in the middle. Other times I was obliged to stay at the bottom, on the level closest to the floor. I know what awaited me there: a stinking pile of filth. I silently accepted everything. Weeping or complaining could be read as a sign of weakness, and would inevitably lead to the end. In Birkenau, you always had to show that you were strong and resolute, not arrogant but alive nonetheless.

My mother came looking for me.

She whispered my name from bunk to bunk.

Luda? she asked in a low voice.

If no one answered, she carried on.

And again she came and asked, *Luda?*

She must have come looking for me every now and again. Even if only to hold my hands and check that I was still there. That while she was at her forced labour Dr

Mengele hadn't taken me away and killed me. Or at least that I had come back to the barrack alive. Damaged perhaps, but alive.

Of course there was no shortage of desperate days. The ones when she came to the barrack and didn't find me. When I wasn't on the wooden boards. She dropped to the brick floor, the only luxury that the adult detainees managed to obtain for our barrack from the SS. Like the others, our barrack had no foundations, but it did have the advantage of a real floor. My mother slipped past the drawings that some of us had done on the damp grey walls. I was nowhere to be found. It was as if I'd disappeared. Then she was told that Mengele had taken me the day before. She left in despair, and came back the next day. Still nothing. She still couldn't find me. On the third day she saw me, apparently unconscious, on one of the boards. I seemed to be in a coma, lying on my back, my body as transparent as glass. Mengele must have stayed his hand, and by some miracle I didn't die.

My mother caressed me, tried to bring me back to life. There wasn't much she could do. But I managed to survive, to wake up in spite of everything. A miracle of life amid days of death and desolation.

━

Thirteen months spent in Birkenau meant experiencing the cold of winter twice, and at other times the sweltering heat of continental European summer. And then the spring, which, in spite of the flowers growing around the camp, among the grass and the ashes of the cremated bodies, could not give us hope. And last it was autumn, bringing the smell of an ending, of death, of the returning cold, the days that promised no future.

I never fully explored the source of the onions, although in retrospect I did have an idea. No food was grown in Birkenau. But my mother was a young and healthy woman and every day she was taken outside the enclosure, past the ovens of the crematoria, to dig the river-bed. Men and women in terrible physical condition were forced to repair dykes along the river, to clear ponds and cut reeds and canes that grew in the surrounding area. The village of Harmęże, not far from the camp, had been cleared by the Nazis. They built a poultry farm there, and produced food to feed the SS. Prisoners sometimes managed to steal some of that food. But I don't think my mother's few onions came from those thefts, so small and yet so important, but from the generosity of Poles who lived near the camp. She herself didn't give me too many explanations. *Take them*, she said, as she offered me the pilfered goods. And I obeyed without question.

My meetings with her, as the war intensified, gradually became rarer and rarer. The same was true of the words that she whispered in my ear, trying not to let anyone hear them, not to attract attention. She asked me insistently to say my name to her, how old I was, where I came from. She wanted me to learn those things so that if she didn't make it, I wouldn't forget who I was – so I wouldn't forget my origins, so I wouldn't forget her, my mother, who brought me into the world, who was the first to kiss me, to cuddle me, to love me. And so that I could tell whoever found me along the way. *My name is Lyudmila, Luda to my family. I'm five years old. I come from Belarus,* I repeated towards the end of our incarceration. She promised me that sooner or later she would take me away. She promised me that it would all soon be over and we would return to our forests, to our land, to our beloved village. But day followed day and nothing changed. The scene that we had witnessed was repeated: the deportees divided into two rows; most of them going to die, a minority surviving. Anyone who tried to rebel was executed on the spot. The Germans were animals, it seemed to us. Just animals. Sometimes they would strip us naked in front of them. Children, women, men, all naked in front of their eyes. They weren't aware that we didn't feel shame. You can't feel shame in front of animals. Naked or clothed, it made no difference to any of us.

When my mother went back to her barrack, I curled up in my own world. A world made up of a silence, my own, which I soon came to understand as the only possible response that we could give to our jailers. Silence was my only chance of survival. I learned it instinctively, without anyone telling me or explaining anything. I had no teachers inside the camp; I had no friends; I had nothing. I was alone with my instincts. I didn't make a sound even when a rat ran over my legs in search of food. When a little boy beside me groaned in the depths of the night and suddenly died. When I was attacked by fleas and ticks. When the SS came and grabbed me to take me to Mengele. It was a silence in which I tried to disappear so as not to die. A silence that I made my own even in the presence of my mother, her face desperate in spite of her attempts to look serene and calm and give me strength. I didn't want to appear weak in her eyes. I didn't want to make her suffer. And I didn't want to suffer either.

I didn't weep; I didn't shout; I didn't ask for anything. I learned to stifle all my feelings. They were alive within me, but they didn't have the right to existence or expression. Anyone who went through a major trauma was either overcome by madness or learned apathy. I chose the latter.

23

The world was passing me by. I just survived, waiting for better times.

When I was seized by longing for my mother, for my father who had stayed in Belarus, for my grandparents who had disappeared in the camp, I stamped it down. I couldn't cry; I couldn't laugh; I couldn't feel anything. My face turned to marble, rigid. And my spirit was the same.

I didn't fully understand what Birkenau was; I didn't know exactly why I was here, why some of us were being killed, why there were no games, smiles, hugs. Why every now and again they would line us up in single file outside the barrack. Why some of us children were selected, taken away and brought to Mengele. I didn't understand most of the things that happened, but rooted deep within me was the intuition that my task was to live, not to die.

Years after Birkenau a journalist asked me if I hated the SS. If I hated the Germans, their words, their uniforms, their evil and violence. If I hated the people who had stolen my childhood. I said no. Luda was, in fact, a little girl who couldn't hate because she couldn't love either. She couldn't feel anything. I had numbed myself so that I could survive the pain, the fear, the absurdity of the world into which I had suddenly been plunged.

In Birkenau I didn't hate; I didn't love; I had no friends or playmates. I had nothing. I tried to stay out of trouble.

I fled from everything; I fled the pain that surrounded me, and by doing that I also escaped to a place within myself. And even today it is this child who comes alive in me. So much so that Luda still struggles to allow herself any feelings, even all these years later. She still tends to hide them. She still believes that she must only survive, that she mustn't show what she feels, what she desires, because her task is to resist and to merely live another day. Even though I must admit that bearing witness helps me. Telling stories helps others to understand what happened, helps the world not to forget, but for me it also involves reliving that period of my life. And at the same time I understand that it wasn't my fault that I had no feelings in the camp. It was a necessary form of defence, the only one possible. That's what Luda was: the little girl who did not know how to – indeed, *could* not – hate. And who could not love either.

I believed in my mother. I believed in her last words before she set off on the death march towards Bergen-Belsen: *remember what your name is and where you come from because I will come back and take you away from here*. It was the end of 1944. I will later discover that at that moment Soviet forces were advancing through Poland towards Birkenau and Auschwitz. Liberation was close. The Germans had understood that their time was up, and had decided to transfer the inmates to other camps in Germany. The trains arrived. They were loaded up. First destination: Wodzisław Śląski, then they would push on ahead, into the heart of Germany. My mother was destined for Bergen-Belsen.

She came to my barrack for a last farewell. She was agitated, worried that she wouldn't be able to see me again. She had no idea what was going to happen to her. And neither did I. We had somehow survived, even though we were surrounded by enemies. For months, at any moment, we could have been killed for the most futile reasons. By a miracle, it hadn't happened. A fate that was both ineffable and also blind, unfair in its randomness, saved us. We were spared despite not having any particular merit. But everything was still in the balance. Anything could happen.

I remember her eyes from that last meeting. They looked at me with love and despair. She held my head in her hands as she looked me straight in the eyes and kissed me. I was her daughter; I was her heart; I was her love. I remember her words. I repeated them for days after she left. *Remember what your name is and where you come from.* I am Luda Boczarowa, I am five years old, I come from Belarus. My maternal grandparents came to Birkenau with me, transported in that big red-brown carriage. On the tracks they were immediately taken away and gassed. They died in a few minutes. My father was taken away by the Russian army before the deportation. My mother was brought to Birkenau with me and then sent towards Bergen-Belsen. Still on the tracks, Dr Mengele chose me. I was small, but in perfect health. I looked older than I was. I was left alone in the camp. My mother wasn't there. She left before the liberation. The Germans have left now too. I have been left alone, but I swear to myself and I swear to God: as long as I live I will look for her; I will try to join her again, to hug her tightly as we did the last time. And I will say the only thing that matters: *I love you, Mama*.

2

T HE GERMAN TRAINS STARTED PUFFING early in the morning on the plains of Belarus, on the border with Poland, after our invasion by Nazi Germany in June 1941. They transported men and weapons. Adolf Hitler was moving his troops to conquer new '*Lebensraum*' in Eastern Europe. My country was important territory, a strategic buffer with the Soviet Union. And we Belarussians were victims of a conflict that didn't belong to us, and once we had been conquered we became foreigners in our own country.

Fear took hold of us in our streets. People increasingly sought refuge in their houses. In the cities the Jews were put in ghettos, walled up in districts that were growing more unsafe by the day, prisons that they could leave only when the SS decided to take them to far-off places.

31

The whistles of the locomotives woke us up at night, and they continued by day. By turns the children hid in the forests along the tracks, to count how many weapons the trains were transporting. And then they would come back to their parents to tell them the information, which was then passed to the leaders of the underground partisan movement.

I remember the puffs of smoke, and how big the iron wheels looked to me, then my friends running breathlessly and passing on the information, the pride in the eyes of the adults. We didn't understand everything, but we felt we were also part of a big plan.

We became partisans. When the Germans invaded and burned our village not far from the Polish border, my parents took me and my maternal grandparents to live in the woods among the great plains. And to collaborate and work for the resistance.

More than anything else, I followed the children who were bigger than me, or else I was in my mother's arms as she ran down the paths along the railway. I hid with her among the leaves and bushes when a train passed. I stayed motionless, lying on the ground. My heart beat madly. And then I came back, part of the group with information to communicate.

Collecting information was, in fact, the only game that

we children played in that early part of 1943, the year that changed my life and the lives of so many of my compatriots for ever. We weren't allowed any others. The whole territory was in the grip of fear. We couldn't afford to have fun or distractions. We were children, but we were treated as adults. And, like the adults, we had to fight to stay alive.

Anna, my mother, was young and indomitable. She had a rebellious nature, as did my father Aleksander. He was reflective, while she was more instinctive, but both immediately understood which side evil was on. The Nazi ideology was the enemy that we had to fight, that we had to resist. In terms of religion, they were both Catholic. Unlike others, they were aware of the Nazi abomination. They didn't compromise with power; they didn't beat about the bush. They had no doubts. They stood against Hitler and Hitler's Germany, and they did their best to resist it. They put themselves on the side of the Jews. Certainly, the Soviet ideology is often run through with anti-Semitism. My family knew that, and lots of partisans knew it too. The challenge was to resist without reaching an accommodation with either of the two sides. To be different, or at least to try to be – that was the maxim for most Belarussians during those difficult months.

My mother often went to observe the trains. She would creep among the bushes along the tracks and listen to the far-off sounds, the voices of the forest, words that she knew how to translate. She could hear the trains arriving before anyone else did. She had a sense for it. She recorded the information on a little piece of paper that she would then hide among my blonde curls. That was why she brought me with her. The risk of bumping into Nazi soldiers was always just around the corner. Usually children weren't checked. Raids were a daily event across the whole of the territory. In the woods we were safer, certainly, but during those months anything could happen at any moment. In the villages of the plain many Jews as well as partisans like us had been captured, and nothing was heard of them again – perhaps they ended up in labour camps for prisoners, beyond the borders, in Poland or Germany. The ghettos were liquidated in only a few days. The inhabitants were flushed out house by house, and taken away by force. Various Jews found refuge in the woods with us. I couldn't tell the difference between us and them because there didn't seem to be one. The grown-ups talked about the violence of the Germans against various groups of people, but for me they were all the same: Belarussians. I observed and, like everyone else, put up with it.

My parents were familiar with all the paths and hiding places. Night and day they moved, agile as deer. They didn't just collect information; they also invited the Jewish families to join them. Having fled the villages, the Jews often found themselves wandering around aimlessly. The risks for them were enormous. The German manhunt had been going for some time. Opposing it was a moral obligation. We had to survive, fight and help the most vulnerable.

Like many other partisans, we lived in a *zemlyanka* – a hole dug in the ground where potatoes were stored during the long winters. Often we had to change *zemlyanka*. Sometimes, in fact, the holes were discovered by the Germans and destroyed. Luckily the sentries on the edge of the forest told us just in time when the enemy were in the zone, so we would quickly leave our refuges and flee. We would try to cover the *zemlyanka* with leaves, but often it wasn't enough. When the Germans found it they destroyed it. We could hear the shouts in the distance. They were furious not to have captured us. We moved to less accessible zones, perhaps marshy and more hostile. Another *zemlyanka*, damper and less welcoming, became our house. My parents were willing to continue this life for as long as it took. For months if necessary. It wasn't a dignified life but at least we were free, still masters of our own lives.

Sometimes we would bump into other small communities of partisans. The most highly developed had set up an infirmary in their surroundings, a school for the children, a synagogue, small shops, in an attempt to recreate in the forest the life they had in the villages. Many survived by trying to cultivate barley or wheat. Some groups were commanded partisans connected to the Soviet Union. My parents tried to be independent. Resist everything and everyone was their motto.

My grandparents were old by now, but they were still in good health. They'd also brought Michał, my brother, into the woods. He wasn't really my brother, but over time that's what he became. He was older than me, about thirteen. My grandparents adopted him before fleeing into the woods. After he lost his father, they took him in to work on their little farm with his mother. It was the woman who insisted and my grandmother who agreed. Michał became like a son to them.

At first, I refused to accept it; I was jealous. My grandmother took me aside and said gently: *Luda, you can't send him away, you can't reject him. Think of him as your big brother.* Now, during our forays into the woods, he would often run ahead of me, leaping and jumping. He was quick and agile. Over time I came to love him and to accept his protection. He taught me to run along the paths with him and run away from fierce animals. And also from the Germans. He taught me how to wade through rivers, how to catch fish in the many little streams. He helped me make a stick to walk more safely. At night he went down with me into the *zemlyanka* and covered me with leaves to protect me from the cold. He soon became a friendly, faithful presence.

My grandmother was a generous woman. She welcomed Michał into the family and for her it was a spontaneous gesture. My mother and father accepted him without any trouble, and over time he became like a son to them too. Among other things an extra pair of hands for the resistance couldn't hurt. The future among the *zemlyankas* was uncertain, although the present was fine in spite of everything. The woods of our Belarus, even in difficult times, somehow offered a warm embrace. Even today, when I find myself walking past certain woods, I am filled with the smells of those days. The wet leaves, the moss at the foot of the trees, the grass in the little clearings open to the sky are friendly scents. I also have images from that time that come to me like lightning bolts: solitary walks at dawn in search of nuts and berries, the first tadpoles in the pools, the hares leaping among the trees, the occasional deer running off in terror among the foliage.

Before Birkenau it was here that my soul was shaped. It was here that it found its first vital force. The darkness of the camp never managed to swallow up entirely the light that filled me in this place. It is thanks to that time in the woods, despite the uncertainty of our lives, that I have always managed to see the positive side of everything. Nature is constantly reborn and says to the heart of man: *you can always start over again; life is always open to a new beginning.* And that certainty has never abandoned me, even if life has not always been simple.

I remember my mother's eyes, cat's eyes in the nights of the resistance. My father's silence as he lit a cigarette at twilight just outside our *zemlyanka*. Then overnight he disappeared: against his will he was enlisted in the Russian army. He was forced to accept it; he had no choice and couldn't say no. He had tried to keep his distance from the Russians as well, but he didn't succeed. At any rate his motto was: never with the Germans. And in his way, he remained true to it.

I remember him waving and going. His last kiss for my mother. There was no fear in his eyes. He told her everything would be fine. Of the two of them, my mother was the stronger, the solid foundation. And by being enlisted my father lost a great support. But the conviction that they would see each other again sustained him. He left us without a fuss.

The enemy was close, sometimes very close. But in our hearts we were sure: they wouldn't catch us; we would win in the end.

Certainly, we were frightened every time there was a German raid. They climbed the slopes, advancing among the trees, speeding over the clearing in their jeeps. Then they would get out on foot, guided by their dogs on leads.

Our sentries observed their movements, hidden among the tall branches. When they worked out that they were heading towards us, they came down and told us where to flee to. We were forced to head into territories that we had never explored.

There were old people with us, and children, which meant that we had to plan our escape. To move too late, or too slowly, could mean being captured. And the Germans were unpredictable. They could take us away and deport us, or even decide to kill us on the spot, without scruple. In their eyes our lives were worthless. They could kill us or let us live on a whim. They had been thoroughly indoctrinated. Hitler, the adults said, maintained that knowledge spoiled the young. An active youth, determined and dominating, was what was needed. And looking into the eyes of those young Germans, that was how they were: ignorant and resolute. They really thought they belonged to a superior race. If you weren't one of them, you were nothing.

One morning a sudden storm masked every sound in the forest. We left the *zemlyanka* and tried to seek shelter under some trees. For weeks we had been living day by day. I don't know how many trains I saw coming along the tracks, how many wagons, how many cannon and weapons on the convoys.

Suddenly one of our sentries appeared. He must have been running like mad and couldn't speak. He got his breath back and said: *the Germans, the Germans are coming*. There was a sudden panic. The youngest and strongest started running in the direction opposite to the one from which the sentry had come. After a few minutes my mother found my grandparents and Michał. We too could try to flee. There was no time to go and collect our belongings.

We followed the stream of people ahead of us. My mother carried me on her back. I could run on my own, but she thought this would be faster. The branch of a tree struck me right on the forehead. I started bleeding. I'd already learned that particularly in emergencies I mustn't make a sound: silence can save you. So I didn't say anything. I held my hand over the wound while my mother ran. Eventually I felt something running along my neck. Something warm. It was my blood. She stopped for a second and worked out what had happened, then wiped me down with the first leaf she found on the ground and started running again, with me on her back. Luckily my injury wasn't serious.

After a few minutes the rain stopped coming down, but we noticed another sound. It was an increasingly loud and powerful one. We crossed a clearing and found ourselves facing a big river, in full flow. There were no escape routes to the right or to the left. We had no other choice but to wade through it. Some were already in. The impetuous waters welcomed them. At one point the current was very strong, and the only way through it was to swim. We were about to get in when a voice behind us shouted: *Halt!* We froze, petrified. They'd got us. There was no point in reacting.

We turned around slowly and instinctively put our hands above our heads.

There were about twenty of them. Armed, with dogs on leads. They enjoyed seeing the terror rising in our eyes.

They came closer. They ordered us to sit on the ground in a circle. Some of them overtook us and pointed their rifles towards the fugitives who were still in the middle of the river. They fired, shooting them in the back. The lifeless bodies slipped across the surface of the water, like bits of wood carried by the current towards the rocks. The ones who fled first died first. We were still alive, but we didn't know for how long.

My mother was the most lucid. Sitting between the mud and the grass, she gave us reassuring glances. She was telling us we had to be quiet, to not provoke the Germans, to follow their orders. And when they asked us to move, to march towards an unknown destination, we had to comply and move our legs to wherever they said. She was determined. She wanted to live. She was not afraid. She even managed to give us a smile.

None of us had ever heard a word about Vitebsk, where we were transported in the train. It wasn't a long journey, but all piled on top of each other, we couldn't breathe. The goods wagon that we were crammed into was dark, and there were no air vents. I felt sick and so did my mother, Michał and our grandparents.

When the train stopped we were dragged out into a terrible-looking reality. Men and women were on their last legs in what had once been a town and was now an open-air prison. We were in the Vitebsk ghetto. Hundreds of Jews and rebels like ourselves were unloaded from the train and made to wait for other destinations, or perhaps to wait for death.

The massacre of 11 October 1941 affected us all. The survivors told us about it. On that day the River Vićba took the lifeless bodies of sixteen thousand Jews massacred by the Germans.

The ghetto was prey to waves of illness. Men and women were constantly dying. There was no food, no water, nothing. Anyone who fell sick was executed, and anyone who didn't risked the same fate. The Germans felt no mercy. In their eyes we were all guilty. Of what? Of not being German.

My mother and grandparents were taken away several times, brought somewhere and questioned. They said nothing to us, but they looked distraught. Escape was impossible. The end seemed imminent for all of us. Most of the others were Jews. We were them. They were us. I was not born Jewish, but I experienced their separation from the world, their annihilation. Fate had decreed that that was how it would be, that I would be Jewish without being Jewish. I didn't understand the reasons for the situation, but I found myself in it with my family.

It might seem strange, but my clearest memories

concern the days that immediately followed our capture and our transfer to this prison-like place. The Germans decided it was time to move us. A train was ready for us at Vitebsk station. They forced us into the wagons. We had nothing to eat or drink. There was no toilet, just a hole in the floor. Like everyone else I had to do my business there, under the eyes of the other prisoners. There was no shame in front of the Germans, but in front of my companions there was.

The journey was endless. I thought of the passing landscape and wondered: *is it possible that no one can see us? No one can stop us? Save us?* There was no sound apart from the wheels on the tracks. When the train stopped for a while there was silence outside. Perhaps these were uninhabited areas, or perhaps fear kept everyone in their own homes. It was as if the trains didn't exist. I dreamed of some kind of attack, an ambush, someone intervening to kill the Germans and free us, but it didn't happen. No one helped us. We were prisoners being herded into nothingness. We were alone in a world entirely indifferent to our fate.

I had never felt so hungry, or so thirsty. Worst of all was the lack of air. It was hideously stifling. The smell inside the wagon was revolting. As the train puffed slowly along, some people fainted; others died. I lost all sense of time. I don't know how many days I spent in there. I could no longer say who I was.

Eventually I let go. I leaned against my mother and, held up by the bodies around us, I fell asleep. My mother found the strength to caress me, to make me aware of her presence. She had an energy that others lacked. She had a strength that was all her own. I think she was also filled with rage at the injustice to which she and our people had been subjected. Her reaction was to fight – it was as if her body was fuelled by fury; as if it gave her an explosive force.

I can almost see her eyes. They were open in the darkness of the train. They gazed into the void but they spoke. They said: *let's see what happens. I'm here, and I'm alive. And I will go on living. Let's see what you can do to me.* It's hard to explain, but her strength was what sustained me, and what would sustain me over the months to come. Knowing that she wasn't afraid. Even though she never expressed her feelings, I could see it in her eyes. I felt that she was indomitable.

Our grandparents were exhausted. They were only a few feet away from us, and Michał was with them. When I woke up I heard them all groaning. I could recognize their breathing among all the others. I was worried that they would die, that they wouldn't make it. I tried not to

45

think about it. To distract myself I concentrated on my grandmother's house, the one where she lived in Belarus before escaping into the woods. She always had a wood fire blazing in the hearth. Potatoes were cooked in the embers, and gave off a heavenly smell. Outside, the grass in a sprawling meadow was stirred by the wind. It seemed that nothing could disturb that peace. I would only understand many years later: not to have taken in Michał would have been too great an affront to a friend. My grandparents had everything: they had peace and they had prosperity. And Michał was to share in that well-being. For them it was a way of giving something back. Of thanking heaven for its blessings. And that's how it was.

The train stopped yet again. All of a sudden the door of the wagon was hurled open. We felt cold, very cold. We dropped out one at a time. Everything around us was white. It was snowing and windy, nature frozen, like our hearts. I didn't know where we had ended up. I would discover later that the place was called Birkenau, an extermination camp in Poland.

The soldiers divide us up into two lines. I look around and can't see my grandparents. There's no light. It's evening, perhaps even night. Either way, it is already dark. The soldiers aim powerful spotlights at us. They can see us. We can't see them very well. In the distance a column of smoke seems to have a slight pink glow. Or perhaps I'm mistaken. We're standing up, tottering. We don't know what to do. How to behave. What to ask. How to beg for help. Grandma and Grandpa aren't with us any more. They've been taken away. I don't understand why. I didn't say goodbye to them. They've gone away. I will soon understand: I'm never going to see them again. I don't know if I imagined it or if I really did see them, but a distant memory shows me two old people walking away with their backs bent, demoralised. They are walking towards their deaths, holding hands to the end.

We are also separated from Michał. He's young and in good health. The Germans can use him as part of the work force. I don't have time to say goodbye to him either. He leaves with some other people.

The camp is enormous. There are dozens of barracks, on either side of the train tracks. I will end up on the left, he on the right. It all happens very quickly. A soldier with perfectly combed-back dark hair comes over to me. He's clean and well dressed. He looks into my eyes for a long time. I think he's struck by the fact that they're blue, like Aryan eyes. I look German. He opens my eyelids then closes them again. He smiles. He feels my arms, then my legs. I'm three years old but I look older. I'm plump, fleshy, in good health. I'm perfect for what he wants.

He orders me to be taken from my mother.

And he chooses me.

I'm his.

I don't know who he is. I will soon find out. They take me to a barracks full of children like me, stacked on top of one another. Piled up on hard wooden shelves. Hands and feet protrude from these shelves, and occasionally you can see furtive, frightened eyes. The children are dirty, filthy. The smell is revolting. I see their eyes. They're inexpressive and apathetic, the eyes of those unfamiliar with light, or who believe that light will no longer be part of their lives. Once we are inside they explain to me: I have been chosen by Dr Josef Mengele in person. I remember that name: Mengele. It's on everyone's lips. Mengele is an inescapable presence. From that day he becomes part of my life. Am I lucky? To some extent yes. He needs me for his experiments, but he needs me alive.

3

M Y MOTHER IS WEARING A KIND OF jacket with blue and grey stripes. Her skirt is blue and grey as well, and she is wearing clogs. Her head is completely shaven. She hugs me and tells me not to be afraid. A few hours have passed since we arrived in Birkenau. They haven't yet separated us. Sitting on her knee, I'm not afraid. I'm not scared. I don't cry. Since the days in the woods of Belarus I've learned to control my feelings. If you show yourself as weak, helpless or in pain, the enemy takes advantage and unleashes his worst instincts against you. On the other hand, if you remain impassive, you may succeed in confusing him; instinctively he may take a step back. The worst people are often insecure. They foam with rage; they shout to hide the fact, mostly from themselves, that they are hesitant. I realize very quickly: the deportees who manage not to show fear have a greater likelihood of surviving than those who show weakness. Of course, in the camp, being strong is difficult, almost impossible. I manage to do it, but not at all deliberately. I don't understand what's happening to me, not really, not entirely. So I survive, in a darkness that envelops me but at the same time doesn't take over me.

The enemy are everywhere. I recognize them all of a sudden. Most of them are tall, blond young men, with white skin without a heart underneath it. Some have moustaches, like Hitler. They're copying their leader. They feel strong in their uniforms. The Nazi credo fills them completely. There is no chance of undermining their view of the world. The only answer to give them is silence. To endure in silence, trying not to die.

That day, as soon as we had arrived in the camp, one of them approached us. He was holding a plate covered with needles. The needles formed a number: mine was 70072, my mother's 70071. I was told to lie down on an iron bed, then to stretch out my left forearm. I held it out bravely. I didn't look at it; I stared into the void. My mother was obliged to stay a few yards away from me. She was powerless. She had to witness what was happening without being able to stop it. Other deportees wrote our numbers down on sheets of paper. Yes, other deportees:

they were the ones who collaborated with the Germans, who helped them, particularly with their dirty work. I would learn that some of them did it because they were forced to, others to gain an advantage. The rule of the survival of the fittest prevailed at the camp. There was no other. There was no solidarity among the deportees, the darkness in there was too great. And the abyss that we were all plunging into together was too big for us to be able to hold each other by the hand.

We no longer had names, just numbers. What the Germans didn't know, however, was that those registers would condemn them. Those numbers written on white sheets of paper with our names next to them would bear witness to our having been there, to our having been tattooed, to the horror that had taken place. It was the Germans themselves who left an indelible record of it all, black ink on white paper. Without realizing it, they were the first witnesses, with their registers of death.

Sometimes the SS became aggressive. They even vented their frustrations on us children, but more often on the grown-ups. My mother soon paid the price. She was caught one day with onions in her hand. They were for me. They raised her chin with their left hand and with their right they punched her in the mouth. Other punches followed, remorselessly. She lost her front teeth, and a lot of blood.

I asked her what had happened. She told me without worrying that I might be shocked. She told me to let me know that I had to be cunning, alert. She hadn't been alert enough, and as a result she had lost her teeth. She was still beautiful, even without them. She was still a beautiful young woman in spite of everything.

The soldier's pressure on the outside of my forearm was swift and decisive. When the needles pierced the flesh I felt pain, but I still managed to contain myself. I didn't pull a face; I didn't cry out or weep. I didn't want to give them anything, any satisfaction. When he gestured to me to get back up, I looked at my forearm and noticed only an indefinable black mark. I would discover that it took time for it to be absorbed so that the numbers 70072 could be clearly read. It would be the only tattoo I ever had. Over time I noticed with the passing of the years that the numbers became bigger and bigger, and more and more legible. For me it would be a sign, once I had reached a certain age, that I had to bear witness: not to hide those numbers, but to tell everyone what had happened.

Another caress from my mother, as if to tell me what a good girl I'd been. Back then I couldn't have imagined what that number would mean for me. In particular I couldn't have had any idea that it would keep me company for years, that even as an old woman it would still be with me, on my skin, ineradicable. Marking things was a German fixation. They marked the Jews in the Vitebsk ghetto. They marked their houses, their clothes. And they marked them inside the camps.

My mother tried to be gentle with me. She stroked my head, then my brow. She looked at me with love. She ran her fingers over the scar that I still had from my injury in Belarus, as we tried to escape the Germans in the woods. She said my name, asked me to repeat it. She was obsessed by the possibility that I might forget it. She told me that my scar had been a blessing. One more distinguishing feature. If we were separated and she had to come and find me, that scar would say who I was. No one could be mistaken, not even – if such a thing was possible – my mother.

In the children's wing, the barracks to which I had been assigned, everyone was like me. Everyone had a number on their arm. No one knew the names of the others. We didn't talk much among ourselves; we didn't communicate. We were more or less in the middle of the camp; there were other barracks around us, but we were on our own. There was terror in everyone's heart. Dirt, so much dirt, on our skin. We couldn't wash – there was no running water. The walls, the wooden boards of the makeshift beds, were full of insects, parasites. They got into our clothes, they lived on our skin, even in our private parts. The more I chased them away, the more they came back. There were rats and filth everywhere.

As if everything wasn't bad enough already, there was the kapo. She was a mean, heartless woman. She wasn't German; she was a deportee like us. She lived in a room by the entrance to the barracks. She had a stick and a whip stored carefully behind her door. She picked up each in turn, and used them to vent her anger on us, furiously, heedlessly. She used them on anyone who made a mistake, or anyone who didn't obey. But she herself was filled with fear. Rather than dominating her, it took her over and turned into anger, which was then taken out on us. If we didn't obey her orders, we were beaten and whipped. According to the Gospels, wailing and gnashing of teeth is the fate of those cast out of the Kingdom of Heaven, those who will not be admitted to the presence of Abraham, Isaac and Jacob and all the prophets, the ones who will not be granted access to Paradise. Birkenau was the reverse. A God who had become mute and incomprehensible seemed to be reserved for the just, the innocent. The unspeakable was taking place, and the unspeakable cannot be described even to Heaven. Later on, I would find my own situation reflected in the words of the Jewish philosopher Hans Jonas: God did not intervene, he says, not because he didn't want to but because he couldn't. Who stopped him? I think it was the evil of men. Against that even God could do nothing but take a step back.

We had no food, only black bread and water. We were given the black bread in the morning. Water was 'sold' to us as soup for dinner. Sometimes they also brought us a kind of coffee made of weeds. It was undrinkable, but we drank it down anyway. It gave us terrible stomach cramps. In these conditions you can get used to anything. And above all you learn that anything can help to keep you alive. The toilets were latrines in which we had to relieve ourselves in front of everyone. There was no shame. There was only humiliation.

Taking part in inspections amid the cold and hunger was a very difficult experience. The most terrifying thing for each of us was that Dr Mengele might choose us. Often he came looking for us. He came right into the barracks. I clearly remember his high-sided boots, black and polished till they gleamed. I remember the sound of those boots on the barracks floor. When he came in I would throw myself on the wooden blanks under the lowest shelf.

I would push myself as far as I could into the corner, on the floor by the wall. I was small, so it was easier for me to get to the darkest and most hidden spots. Other children did the same. The ones who weren't fast enough to hide or couldn't get under the shelves risked being caught. Anyone who was caught ended up in the laboratory on the other side of the camp.

Sometimes Mengele would come and get us early in the morning when it was still dark outside. Then I would close my eyes. *If I can't see him, he can't see me,* I thought. Many other children did the same thing, covering their faces with their hands. They were alone with a terror that they should never have had to face. Trying to disappear was the only way to endure the nightmare in which we found ourselves. We were children who didn't have nightmares at night because nightmares walked with us always, at every moment. Our lives were the worst nightmare that it was possible to imagine. Alone, without our parents, trapped in revolting barracks with evil kapos keeping watch over us, with the spectre of the experiments, the spectre of death. The ones who were chosen didn't always come back. The ones who were chosen could also die, could also end up in nothingness. When, at the end of each day, one of us didn't come back, we looked towards the ovens of the crematoria. We all thought the same thing:

our companions no longer exist; they have become smoke and ash and dust in the air.

Sometimes the inspections were outside the barracks. The kapo told us to leave quickly. We stood in a line. She inspected each of us in turn. Read the tattoo numbers on our forearms and signed us off as present with her pen in a notebook. At the end of the inspection someone was always missing. When that happened, she would go back into the barracks with other SS members and after a few minutes she would come out holding the missing child. They were dead. If someone didn't respond to the call to inspection, it wasn't because they were hiding or because they had decided not to come out. No, if they didn't reply, they were already dead. I don't remember any inspections in which we were all present. Every time it was discovered that someone hadn't made it. Perhaps they'd been sleeping beside you that night, perhaps they tried to find a place on the boards asking you to shift up. And then in the morning they weren't there: an illness, or simply malnutrition, had carried them off.

The kapo called me *Jüdin*, even though I wasn't; I don't know why. Every now and again my mother would come and find me and remind me who I was, so that the memory of my past would stay with me should I manage to survive. She wanted me to be aware of my past. Of my history.

59

She knew that I could die. That between the two of us I was the more likely to make it. And she knew that thanks to me something of her might live on too, something of her past, something of what she had been and of what she had left in this life. For that reason, she insisted on making me repeat my name, the place I came from, the town where I was born. My roots were hers; my roots were what would be left of her if she didn't survive. For that reason, she kept caressing my scar, and making me repeat: *I am Luda, daughter of Belarussian partisans, deportee to Birkenau. I am Luda, the little girl with a scar on her forehead.*

When they called me *Jüdin* I didn't react. If I spoke, if I told them I wasn't Jewish, it only made them all the more furious. No, it was fine. I was Luda, a Jew by adoption. Fate had decreed that I must become one of them – their daughter, their sister, their relative. You aren't a Jew by birth alone; you're a Jew also because you're forced to experience the same fate as them on this earth.

The days passed monotonously. We couldn't leave the barracks. We were forced to stay locked up in there. We spent hours sitting on the wooden shelves, legs dangling. We rocked our heads silently back and forth. I would later discover that some children in orphanages have this kind of behaviour. Perhaps rocking is the sign of a wound that they don't know how to confront. We rocked ceaselessly.

Our lives were one great wound. When the kapo came and called us for inspection we jumped to our feet, but then we resumed our rocking. We couldn't run in the meadows just outside the camp; we couldn't run after butterflies or roll in the grass. We were prisoners of the SS and all our obsessions and fears. We all rocked together, one great ship lost in a hostile ocean.

Soon my body was covered with pustules. Mengele, when he chose me and had me brought to him, gave me blood transfusions. There were other children around me, some bearing marks of violence so deep that I am certain they had little time to live. I was often unconscious when I was brought back to the barracks. It took days for me to recover completely. If the fact that I looked older than I was probably saved my life on the day I arrived in Birkenau, now, on the contrary, it seemed like a double-sided blade. In fact, if I looked healthier and sturdier than the others, Mengele was all the more likely to choose me; he could operate on me whenever he liked. And that was not a good thing. He had no scruples; he had no feelings for anyone; he felt no pity; he was quite clear in the pursuit of his goals.

My mother wanted me to become invisible but knew it wasn't possible. She talked to me in our language, but also tried to make sure that I learned a little German. If

I knew the language of the enemy, I would have a weapon to defend myself with, she told me, to understand what to do in any situation. Sometimes she sensed that I was on the brink of collapsing. Sometimes she noticed that I was close to tears. She caressed me, but then told me to stop it, saying that otherwise the kapo would pick up her stick and beat me. And I believed her and stopped whimpering.

Children have incredible strength when they are forced into difficult situations. There were lots of them living with me in Mengele's barrack. No one would say that we could find the energy needed to survive in there. Yet most people did survive. In fact, we were forced to live our lives as if we were adults in children's bodies. Our childhood had been stolen from us. But soon we would come up with our own strategy to keep us from dying. We were animals, and as such we had an innate instinct for survival. And if it was true that we didn't help each other, it was also true that, at least as far as I could see, we didn't abuse our power over one another. It was every man for himself. That was the simple rule of the camp. We were forced by the absurdity of events to become monads, little beings isolated from everything and everyone within a nightmare world. When Mengele came in and we tried to hide, the law of the swiftest prevailed. The one who was quickest found the best hiding place. The others were left behind. Everyone wanted to be the first to leap away. It wasn't badness or carelessness. It was the toughness of the camp that had made us like this. *Mors tua, vita mea* – the ancient medieval phrase still applied in the middle of the twentieth century.

The laboratories of the Angel of Death, as he would later become known, were near the crematoria. Mengele and his cohorts, other doctors whose names I don't remember, worked with a smile on their lips while a few feet away from them the flesh of innocent men and women burned at extremely high temperatures. If a child didn't survive, they would end up in the ovens, unmourned. All visits by children to the laboratories were recorded. My number can be found in the register of the SS Hygiene Institute. Mine along with many others.

Apart from the transfusions, I was injected with various types of poison. Mengele wanted to see how my body would react. Beside me were the corpses of children who didn't survive. I was living in a nightmare which became a normality day after day. I had not lived for long enough to realize that normality resided elsewhere. I had spent too short a time in Belarus for the days in Birkenau not to become normality in my eyes. Certainly, the woods of Belarus had been a place of light. But the darkness of

Birkenau was so deep that it was as if that light, although it existed, had been temporarily extinguished.

Another thing that soon became normal was the constant stinging in my eyes. When I went to Mengele I was put to sleep, so that when I came out I wouldn't remember exactly what had happened. I would wake up and my body would talk to me and tell me stories. Apart from the pustules resulting from the transfusions and the poison injected into me, the stinging in my eyes told me what had been done. Mengele was obsessed with eyes. I was his favourite guinea pig. He would put liquids into my eyes and see what reactions they provoked. Throughout the days that followed my eyes would sting, and I would often be feverish.

I don't remember the first time I saw Mengele's face. To be honest, his face has faded from my memory. I can't focus on it; I can't keep it in mind. If I look at a photograph of him in the present day, as soon as I look away he evaporates into nothingness. It's as if my brain is refusing to remember him. I think it's something unconscious but at the same time real: a defence mechanism. I only clearly remember one thing about him apart from his gleaming boots: in some remote corner of my mind his cold gaze returns to me. I can't focus precisely on his features. If I had to put them back together in some way, I wouldn't be able to. And yet the sensation of that gaze is alive in me. Even today every now and again it's as if he had come back to look at me. Panic takes hold of me. It's a feeling I wouldn't wish on anyone. He looks at me and says: *you're mine. I can do whatever I want with you.*

Mengele had no feelings for us. He had none for me. Along with my fellow inmates I was only material for his experiments. In front of him all we could do was hold our breath and wait for everything to pass, for the experiment to finish so that we could return to our own barrack. Even that horrible place was desirable when you were with him. The body knew that it was heading for terrible pain. And it also knew that it would want to do nothing but flee.

There were no words in the barrack. It was always dominated by a strange silence. There were no plants, nothing fanciful. There was nothing. We were voiceless children, children used for the filthiest kind of work. Like carrying the bodies of people who had died in the camp to the crematoria. Luckily I was never asked. I was too small to lift a stretcher with one or more corpses on it. But some of the older children were asked. If they said no, they were whipped. They always complied with the order. So the children became morticians. To make matters even worse, they often fell ill because there were still parasites and diseases on the bodies. Sometimes there were dozens of bodies piled up. Sometimes death stood right beside us like a playmate.

I remember one day, towards evening, music reached my ears. In the distance I thought I could hear *'Wir Leben Trotzdem'*, 'We live, nevertheless.' A girl older than me told me that it was some women, some of our women, who had picked up instruments, violins, mandolins, guitars and flutes, to play for the deportees when they came back from forced labour. They had to walk in time to the music. She told me she'd seen them playing when the convoys with the new deportees turned up. She told me that someone, hearing the music, had raised a hand in greeting. Perhaps they thought that since there was music Birkenau couldn't be that bad a place. She explained to me that it was all a tactic. The music was used to lead the new arrivals to the gas chambers while taking away the idea of reacting or even fighting to defend their own lives.

There was also a hospital at the camp. In fact, more than a hospital, it was the antechamber of the crematorium; many sick people died there without receiving any kind of treatment. On some of these the SS completed experiments that were almost always lethal. If they survived, they were gassed.

In one wing of the hospital there was a department for children. Behind two big screens, a paediatrician, very famous in our country, she herself deported shortly after me, was in charge of the children's section. She was an energetic woman, respected even by the SS. It was thanks to her that I didn't die during my detention. One day I woke up with a terrible fever. I felt ill. The kapo sent me to hospital. The doctor discovered that I was Belarussian and asked for information about me. She wanted to know who I was, where exactly I came from and asked if my parents were in the camp. She discovered that my mother had been assigned to forced labour, and persuaded the SS to move her to cleaning duties in the hospital. That way she could be closer to me. We were in close contact for a few days. The doctor protected us. She said I would get better very soon.

But one morning some terrible news arrived. The SS had decided to clear the hospital completely; everyone who had recovered there was to be gassed immediately, killed. There were no discussions, not even the doctor's authority could do anything. My mother acted instinctively, without thinking. She and the doctor wrapped me in a blanket and had me carried out by one of the cleaners. He had to pretend he was throwing away some rubbish. This friend, whose name I don't know, hurried to comply. He left the hospital with this bundle in his hands. The SS watched him but didn't stop him. He managed to carry me to the children's barrack and save my life. By now I was almost cured of my illness. The kapo took me back in as if nothing had happened. I was safe. It was a miracle. I was alive.

4

I KNOW SOME PEOPLE MIGHT SAY THAT I WAS too young to remember. Not so, in fact. I have gathered together the few memories that are still vivid in my mind. I lined them up one by one. Then I connected them with the people who were in the camp with me and who remembered things that I went through there. Last of all I closed the circle by inspecting the archives. And recording where and how my camp number appears. It all matches up.

Snow and wind lashed the camp. For days we had heard cannon fire in the distance. A far-away, constant rumble. *Someone's fighting*, we thought. We also imagined how nervous the Germans must be during those days in late January 1945. Birkenau was immersed in a state of profound desolation, not only due to death, hunger, privations. But the gloom brought on by the cold made everything difficult and impervious. Nature was dead. The night frosts rendered every foray out of the barrack almost impossible. The bodies of the dead, thrown into their holes, became slabs of ice, their faces fixed in stony grimaces of pain. The end surrounded us. It was the end of everything, the end of the world.

I have an image in my mind – I don't know if it's from that winter or the previous one. It's a hole full of corpses. Their faces are transfigured by pain. We walk past them in a line, all children. No one is frightened. That image is something normal to us. Those corpses are our daily life.

The exhaustion is indescribable. First it attacks the body. Day after day it leaves it more and more defenceless. The muscles evaporate, the bones protrude sharply beneath an ever-thinner layer of skin. Our eyes become enormous, bulging from the angularity of our skulls. Our cheekbones look as if they're about to explode. The disfigurement of the body passes directly to the soul. It too yields, day after day. It can't keep itself alive. It lets itself go. Just as death may seem at moments like a blessing. It never is, in fact, but at times it may look like the only salvation, basically the lesser evil. Allowing ourselves to die so that the void will come and take us, removing us from pain that has become unbearable.

That was the message in the eyes of those who were still alive in Birkenau. We couldn't go on. We couldn't put up any resistance to all the things going on around us.

There was considerable agitation among the Germans. It seemed as if something important was about to happen at any moment, but we couldn't work out exactly what. The kapo kept a close eye on the movements of the soldiers. She was nervous too, constantly going in and out of her room, even harsher than usual with us, impatient with everything. The wait was draining because no one understood exactly who or what was on the way. Rumours circulated. There was talk of the Red Army coming to liberate us, of battles on the Polish border. We listened, but we didn't dare to hope. By now we were indifferent to anything that might happen in the future. Let the liberation come and wake us. But let it be as light as a breath of wind. We wouldn't have been able to bear anything more.

The days became even more monotonous. Darkness became our normality. I don't remember any weeping, or any laughter. I think that was the experience of all of us in there. Mothers no longer came in search of their children. My mother no longer came to me. There had been no sign of her for several days. There were no words, no explanations. She just didn't come any more. That was just how it was.

Dr Mengele also stopped coming. He had vanished into nothingness. We heard nothing more of him, of his experiments, of his hospital with its smell of death and blood. He didn't even send his emissaries. The last couple of twin children had been taken away some weeks before. They didn't come back. Rumours in the camp said that they had been killed, their bodies eviscerated after exhausting experiments with medical tongs and injections. The corpses dissected and the internal organs removed and then sent to the Institute of Biological and Racial Research in Berlin, and analysed there with a view to discovering a substantial difference between the blood of Aryans and the blood of Jews. A difference of race, they said. A difference that we, among the prisoners, on the side of the Jews, could not understand. We rocked back and forth on the shelves in our barracks. We were weary, exhausted by months in the camp, by death and pain. We had all entered a dulled state of apathy. Many of us wouldn't have put up any resistance if we'd been taken away to be tortured.

The weariness was great, and opened the way for unimaginable degrees of despair and resignation. We saw adults from other barracks deciding to end it all. They made their way to the perimeter fence, leaned against the electric wires and died. Others didn't respond to the cries of '*Halt*' from the Germans and were mown down by machine-gun fire. They wanted only to finish it all. They wanted only to die.

Some of the Germans became even more malicious. The orders they gave in their language weren't immediately understood. It seemed that they were deliberately yelling unintelligible instructions before laughing at our baffled expressions. Anyone who failed to obey their orders was punished. But what orders? What exactly were they asking us to do? We could only guess, speculate, and some things we inevitably got wrong. Blows came raining down on us out of nowhere. We considered ourselves lucky if we were beaten without being killed.

The wake-up gong sounded as always at four in the morning, however dark it was outside, however bitter the cold. Amid kicks and curses we immediately had to leave the shelves on which we lay. We were driven outside to the communal toilets, where we relieved ourselves as quickly as we could. Breakfast, if one could call it that, was only for the people who made it to the kitchen first. Turnip soup, a broth with a few turnips floating in it. That was the beginning of hours of nothingness, until the final evening inspection.

Another night in our barrack. The kapo told us to go to sleep. She wanted silence; she wouldn't allow sounds of any kind. When she left, the barrack fell into the most total darkness. We could still hear some far-off cannon fire. It was our only lullaby. *Boom, boom*, we heard in the cold of night. Who could guess what was happening out there. Who could guess who was winning, whether the rumble of the cannon would bring death or life.

It didn't occur to anyone to go outside. The SS were still doing their rounds. To go outside would have meant certain death. During those months we witnessed summary executions. We saw people bumped off for pointless reasons. We saw deportees who had tried to flee at night. It should be pointed out that no one succeeded. Every death was senseless here. And it was terrible. Some children remembered the deaths of their mothers, who had been killed in front of them. Others remembered women arriving pregnant in Birkenau. They had been put to death immediately, mown down in front of everyone. The same fate was reserved for the babies who had arrived on the trains. Some were executed immediately after leaving the wagons, torn from their mothers' breasts, others killed immediately afterwards and then burned in the ovens. The Germans killed without thinking. They killed without remorse. They killed because they had been taught that it was the right thing to do. The world was upside down. Evil had become normality. Goodness no longer had the right to exist. I recall the most terrible executions as part of everyday life.

Occasionally, whispering could be heard on the shelves in the barrack. Sometimes someone would say something under their breath. Someone else would moan. The ones who had died during those months had been replaced by living bodies. The movement from life to death was a swift cycle in Birkenau, a ruthless carousel that paid heed to no one.

At one point the walls and windows of the barrack shook. A couple of explosions that seemed to be getting closer. But then they moved away again. Booms that came and went and made everyone nervous. They were the background noise to those weeks, the musical score that marked the end of Birkenau.

An SS man suddenly stormed into the barrack. He hammered the ground with his heels and clutched his whip, ready to strike. The kapo was standing to attention. Then came the command: *Out, everyone, out, right now!*

Why? What's happening? What are they going to do to us? my companions wondered confusedly. We had been about to go to sleep. Now we had to get up and go outside without the luxury of discussing the matter.

Evacuation! the kapo shouted. And again: *Get out, quick, get into a column!*

Some sick children couldn't get up, and stayed where they were. Some were uncertain about what to do. Whether to go or to stay. Whether to pretend to be ill. Many decided it was better to get up. Too often those who were sick came to a bad end. Often the inmates who didn't follow orders wound up dead.

Perhaps I will see my mother, I remember thinking. *Perhaps I'll see her.*

The snow was falling copiously. Big flakes got in our eyes, settled on our shaven heads, covered our filthy clothes, froze our hearts and froze our blood.

They counted us in turn. Then they went into the barracks and counted the children who were ill. We stood there for what seemed like endless minutes. They inspected our tattoos. Some of us, on the point of fainting, were supported by our neighbours. And then, for no reason that we were aware of, they told us to go back inside. We went back in and climbed exhaustedly onto our shelves. Why had they held an inspection? I'll never know. Dawn arrived soon. A new pointless day was about to begin.

All of a sudden the camp was demobilized. The Germans began to destroy the gas chambers, numbers two and three, which were still standing, or at least tried to. Some of the frailer prisoners were executed. Their bodies were piled up all over the place, at random, not least outside our barrack. There were mountains of corpses, mountains of our sisters and brothers who didn't make it. Beside them were their clothes, shoes, their striped uniforms abandoned in the snow. Some people were gathering near the camp gates, at least that was what we were told.

Something had definitely changed. Something new was happening. The bigger children brought fresh information. They said that the Russian soldiers were arriving. They said they were coming to free us. And that the Germans planned to leave with anyone who was still capable of enduring the cold. They said that we were about to start marching. They wanted to head towards Germany, to a safer country. Essentially, they were planning to flee.

I couldn't see my mother.

I didn't know where she was.

I peered out through the chinks in the barrack wall to see if I could find her. I couldn't see her anywhere. I thought she must have left too. It was perhaps the most anxious moment of my time in Birkenau.

She's gone?

She's leaving me here?

Mama, where are you?

I can't survive without you, I can't live.

Two powerful explosions knocked us over. For a few moments we went out into the open. Two big clouds of smoke emerged from the ovens of the crematoria. The second and third had been blown up. Kanada, the barracks area that was used for storage, was set alight as well. We would soon find out: it was the end of the presence of the Germans in Birkenau.

One march set off during the night, and a strange and gloomy silence settled on the camp.

Overnight, it had emptied completely. There were no longer any Germans there. Our kapo had disappeared, vanished into thin air. And yet still we waited. We stayed in the barrack. The snow had turned to ice. Outside there was a white wasteland that none of us had any intention of exploring.

Where could we go?

We hear voices. The Russians are in the camp. They've opened the gates with the help of their horses. Four of them at first, only four. There is no sign of a celebration; no trumpets, no fanfares. All around there is nothing but death and destruction. And death and destruction dwell in the hearts of the few survivors who were not taken away by the Germans.

None of us children leave the barrack. We have no

business out there. We don't clearly understand that the liberation has begun, that we are no longer slaves. We don't have the strength to understand.

Another night passes. In the morning we hear different voices: Polish voices. Residents of nearby Oświęcim – Auschwitz to the Germans – have turned up. They've come out of curiosity, but also in a spirit of solidarity. They want to give us food; they want to support us, help us. Some of us bring out our own bowls. The Russians pour something into them. Many of us try to eat, but some can't even hold a spoon in their hands. So they eat by poking their fingers in and sucking them. One soldier is holding a piece of bread. Some of the inmates grab it out of his hand, weeping, and hug him at the same time.

Eventually we will find out what happened. The Soviet troops advanced quickly, covering 170 kilometres in twelve days, breaking through four German lines of defence and repelling two counter-attacks. The SS guarding the camp received the order to destroy all proof of their presence. Crematorium IV had already been demolished in October 1944. In the last days of December, squads consisting of 150 women and 200 men were used to erase the traces. Covering the holes where the bodies had been burned with grass, removing the ashes and throwing everything into the Vistula. The Germans even ordered them to take away the blood-drenched sand. Many things disappeared for ever.

On 21 December 1944, Birkenau's electrical plants and watchtowers were dismantled. The barrack where the prisoners undressed right by the gas chamber adjacent to Crematorium II was removed. The Germans, aware that the Russians were at the gates, got to work speedily, to recycle everything possible. Part of the ovens and other equipment were dismantled and sent to Lower Silesia, to Gross-Rosen camp. The records of arrivals and deaths and everything that was accumulated as a by-product of the killings had been burnt. And parts of the storerooms were burnt as well.

That was what happened before the Russians arrived.

We could tell who was Russian, or rather who wasn't German, by the uniforms that they wore. They were different from the Germans, and had a red star on their helmets. And also, as far as they could, these soldiers smiled. It wasn't easy for them to smile because they too were dismayed by the terrible cruelty of the camp. They didn't know what to say. They couldn't grasp such madness. They gave us a cup of coffee, warm milk, bread with margarine, a taste that was new to me.

I tried to ask about my mother. I asked if anyone had seen her.

No one knew anything. No one could tell me anything.

It was strange not to see the Germans around us. We were free but we couldn't really understand it.

Some of the barracks were deserted. In others there were still a few people who shyly appeared. Two boys in the distance were carrying the corpse of one of their relatives towards a hole. They gave him a makeshift funeral. There was still a little life in that huge expanse of death.

I heard the voices of soldiers speaking German to some Polish women. They were saying: *Take this child because her mother is dead.*

I understood that they were talking about me. My mother was dead? I couldn't believe it.

A woman approached. She was wearing a black sealskin fur. I touched the fur and hugged it. So warm! So soft!

She asked me straight out: *Will you come with me?*

I said *yes*, without thinking too much about it.

Will you be good? she asked.

Again I said *yes*.

You can guard my geese, she said. *Does that suit you?*

Yes, I said, although I didn't really understand what guarding geese involved.

But then I plucked up the courage and asked: *Have you seen my mother? Have you seen her, by any chance?*

She didn't know what to say. *The soldiers say she's dead*, she said at last, nodding to me to look a little way away.

There was a pile of corpses a few yards away. And I thought she might be there, buried under those bodies. For the first time I realized that there was a possibility that my mother no longer existed. But deep in my heart I didn't think it was so. Deep inside I went on hoping.

The women were all very different. They said they were sent by the priest of Oświęcim. He sent them to us because we had nobody, because we were orphans now. And we needed a family.

I don't know why that woman chose me out of everyone. I was emaciated, and my legs were so frozen that they were red and swollen. I was barefoot, shoeless. I was dirty, filthy, hairless. I was a rag, a scrap that could barely walk.

I got to my feet and made as if to follow her. Then, instinctively, I started crawling. I was scared that someone might see me. In fact, no one was paying me any attention. I could follow the woman without fear. I could walk, just about, with my head high. I could move in any direction. If I wanted to, I could even go walking around the camp on my own. I had the right; I had the freedom. The German watchtowers were empty. There were no machine guns pointing at me. There were no dogs, with their constant barking.

The soldiers with the red stars had stopped paying us much attention, but they did observe us with curiosity, and they observed everything that was going on around them. They must have been stunned by what they saw, an expanse of barracks, most of them abandoned. The signs of what had been there were clearly visible. The flight of the Germans left behind many traces of what had happened. They might have fled, but they weren't able to erase the horrors that they had committed.

Other children were chosen. Other women from Oświęcim were there to adopt us. Just to get away from the camp, we would leave with anyone. We didn't know who they were. They smiled at us. Those smiles, after months of darkness, revived our souls and invited us to be trusting. But we still couldn't drag ourselves out of our unhappiness. We were unhappy even in spite of the liberation. The long-desired end of the darkness had come, but the light around us was different from the one we had imagined.

My light was my mother. It was with her that I would have wanted to leave Birkenau. With her that I would have wanted to return to life. I imagined the two of us taking the train that had brought us here. Travelling back along those tracks together. Climbing into a railway carriage with her to return to Belarus: a normal carriage, not a goods wagon. With something hot to eat and drink in front of us. The Polish plains rushing past the window, our homeland getting closer and closer.

We would travel together to see my grandparents and my brother. We would all live together again. We would go together to our grandparents' house, to the village where we were born. We would light the fire and put the potatoes to cook in the embers. Everything would go back to the way it was before. I would have my teenage years ahead of me and resume the most beautiful years of my life. My father would come home from the war as well. We would be pampered by our country, praised for our resistance. I would run through the fields with Michał. We would go fishing together in the streams. He would carry me on his shoulders when I got tired. I would lie down in the middle of the grass and take great breaths of the clean air of my village. At night I would look at the stars and talk to the moon. I would play the games with the other children that I hadn't been allowed to play in Birkenau.

The camp would be nothing but a distant memory that would gradually fade away. In the evening my mother would put me to bed. She would lie down beside me, hold my hand and sing a lullaby. She would kiss me. I would grow up with my parents, go to the village school, take communion classes in church. I would fall in love and get married. I would have a happy life and the darkness, day by day, would subside. Perhaps I would even forget it all.

That was how my life would be after the extermination camp, after Dr Mengele and his atrocious experiments. I would come out of the gates of Birkenau straight into Belarus, passing beneath the entrance towers looking to the east, towards my beloved country. That's how things would be. That's how I imagined my future at night, on the stinking shelves of the children's barrack in Birkenau.

And instead here I was.

Frightened, I followed a woman with a black seal-skin fur coat who walked smoothly in front of me. She had chosen me. I was hers. She was impatient for me to follow her to her home. She talked to me in Polish, giving me to understand that this would be my language from now on. The camp no longer existed; it had ceased to exist. But not even Belarus existed any more.

On the one hand I was relieved: I was leaving Birkenau; I was getting away from that madness. On the other hand my heart was frozen. My mother wasn't there any more. I wasn't so young that I didn't understand. None of the things that I left in the woods of Belarus would ever be returned to me. I had no news of my father, or my brother or my paternal grandparents. Where were they? I had no answers. And this woman certainly couldn't supply them. I had to go on surviving as I had always done. I only had to blow away the pain that came from my memories. And resist; always resist.

I left the camp on foot. Just as I learned to hide my feelings from the Germans, I did the same with the woman who had chosen me. I neither laughed nor cried. I swallowed back the longing that assailed me on all sides. Longing for my mother; a wrench that tore me apart. I dissembled. I left Birkenau with this woman and I pretended that longing didn't exist.

My name is Luda, the name my parents gave me. My name is Luda, I think, but who I am in reality no longer makes sense. I guess I've been taken because I'm young, younger than all the other children in the camp. Given my age, it's more likely that I will forget, that I won't remember, that a new life will begin as if nothing had ever happened. It's not true; it can't be true, but the illusion remains. Certainly, something new is opening up for me. Something unknown, something that could take me who knows where.

Beneath the entrance arch of Birkenau, beneath the big tower from which the Germans checked the movements of the trains, and from which they directed operations in the camp, I tread on the snow trodden by the deportees forced to flee only a few hours before. The footprints of the great march, which I would discover was a death march, had turned to ice. I put my foot in those prints, trying to find one that resembled my mother's. Perhaps she wasn't dead, I thought again. Perhaps she was one of those who had had been forced to flee.

I slipped on the ground and looked instinctively around: where would the blows from the Germans come from? And then, once again, I realized that the Germans weren't there. There was this Polish woman beside me. She helped me get to my feet, and gestured to me to follow her. Her house wasn't far, she said. The geese were waiting for us. A life together was waiting for us.

My life outside the camp.

5

OŚWIĘCIM, THE CITY THAT ADOPTED me after I left the extermination camp, has a long history. The first settlements date from around the eleventh century, in a place that seemed particularly propitious. The River Sola flows from the Beskydy Mountains with its fresh, clean water, to reach the Vistula. If you had the right sort of boat, you could take your goods to far-off cities: Krakow and then Warsaw. Generations of the town's inhabitants would never have imagined that it would one day become a place symbolizing the greatest human tragedy that had ever happened. That the people of a neighbouring country would take it over and rename it Auschwitz. It seemed like a blessed territory. It wasn't.

And yet there had been some forewarnings of the devastation to come, as if the fate of Oświęcim had been written in the stars. Like many Polish towns, Oświęcim had a story of invasions, the most devastating being the one by the Swedes in 1655. A few decades later, the city was hit by plague and a big fire. It took almost 200 years for Oświęcim to recover. There it stayed, hanging in the heart of Europe waiting for better times.

Those times seemed to begin in the mid-nineteenth century. Oświęcim became a major railway hub on the Krakow–Vienna line. Modernity brought with it work in the factories: a tannery, the Prague-Oświęcim consortium of mechanical engineering and car manufacturing, Jakub Haberfeld's vodka and liqueur business, a fertilizer factory and the Ostryga and Atlantic fish-canning company. And then there was the Potega-Oświęcim agricultural machinery factory. But the plague of floods and fires resumed: in 1863 a fire devastated two thirds of the city, including the tower of the parish church, two synagogues, the city hall and a hospital for the poor.

In the twentieth century, however, after the annexation of Poland to the Third Reich, Oświęcim, like the rest of the country, was subjected to the will of Hitler and his henchmen. And it was chosen as the site of a death factory: one of the extermination camps that the Nazis had called for. Not just any camp, but the one destined for the most terrible notoriety: Auschwitz.

My adoptive parents, the Rydzikowskis, lived on the edge of the city. After the invasion, the land that they owned was expropriated unceremoniously. It was there, in fact, that the Germans decided to build the big gate to Birkenau camp, with its tower.

Of course, they were not alone in suffering that fate: many Poles were deprived of their homes. They were all forced to seek makeshift accommodation elsewhere. The Germans built the barracks of the camp with the materials from those houses. With those bricks they built the new dwellings of the deportees, while their furniture became the doors and their fixtures the windows.

Nothing remained of the old Rydzikowski property. They now lived in a flat in a little block in Oświęcim, as decreed by the Germans. On the evening of my arrival, I found everything new and difficult. All of a sudden I had moved from the shelves of the children's barrack to a clean bed with cool white sheets and a soft pillow.

Before I went to sleep I was put in a basin full of water and soap. Or at least that was the plan. I was about to be washed, but I wasn't used to it. I thrashed about and tried to get away, to escape – I refused to stay still, and water splashed all over the floor. An earthquake had arrived in the Rydzikowski household. An old lady, a friend of the woman who adopted me, had to intervene. They tried to hold me by force. I could feel their hands gripping my arms. I somehow ended up in that blessed bath. I was dried with a big white cloth and then put to bed, but I still couldn't lie still. Again I thrashed around. The two ladies sat on either side of the bed, imagining that I might go to sleep quickly. When they worked out that that wasn't what was happening, they tried to persuade me. I didn't understand everything they said. My eyes darted constantly from one side of the room to the others, my pupils like fireflies going on and off in the darkness of summer nights.

Hours passed, and still I couldn't get to sleep. I was exhausted when, with the first lights of dawn, I collapsed into deep but unsettled sleep. That was how I spent my first night in a normal house. The first night after the woods of Belarus and the barracks of Birkenau. The first night in the Rydzikowski home.

'Pani' – Mrs, or madam – was what I called the woman who took me out of the camp. I couldn't call her 'Mama', or even by her name, Bronisława. She herself didn't ask me to, at least not for now. I would discover that she was married, but that her husband Ryszard was still in a German labour camp in the heart of the Third Reich. He was one of many Poles who had been taken from their homes and sent to forced labour.

The lady didn't talk about him very much, and her

manners were brisk. She tried to be nice to me. She often was, although sometimes she could prove to be rather harsh. She put on a kind of shell, a hard exterior that made it impossible to get through to her. I would come to understand a lot of things about her later on. For now, what I could see was only a bossy woman forcing herself to be what nature had never allowed her to become: a mother.

She talked to me in Polish, a language that I would learn quickly. There were lots of Polish Jews in the camp, and I had somehow learned to decipher some of their whispered language. So the lady's first words weren't entirely alien to me: go to sleep now, eat, don't run, stand still. Her commands were nicer than those of the Germans, but at the same time they were bossy. I went along with them too. My mother had taught me: if you want to survive, disappear, say nothing and – most importantly – don't react. Do as you're told and you won't have any problems.

So I soon adapted, and silently complied with the woman's orders. But I was a very active child, always wanting to play and unused to living in a normal house. Keeping me quiet, getting me to eat meals without making a mess, getting me to go to sleep at specific times was an ongoing battle for the lady. I maintained my composure even when the reproaches became unbearable: often she would threaten to take me back to the camp in order to get me to do what she wanted. *Do you want to end up back in there?* she would ask me. *Weren't the beatings the Germans gave you quite enough?* On those occasions I didn't reply or react, but at the same time I didn't feel afraid. She didn't frighten me, and the camp didn't frighten me either. I'd been told it was now completely empty: what was there to be afraid of?

I would have to say: after what I'd seen in Birkenau I was no longer afraid of anything. My life seemed to be settling now. And yet in the depth of my heart, particularly at night, a faint yet terrible longing fell upon me: *Mama, where are you? Mama, come and get me.* I would repeat those words under my breath, looking at the sky, at the stars and the moon, from a window in my room. Was my mother looking at them too? I wondered. *I will never forget who I am. I'm Lyudmila, your little Luda.*

The morning after my arrival, I woke up groggily. I had finally got to sleep, but I wasn't rested. I couldn't work out where I was. Then I collected my thoughts: the liberated camp, the lady with the black fur, the invitation to follow her along the snowy path, the cold, and then the new house with its warmth and that soft bed from which I leap as if I still had to take part in the kapo's morning inspection. I furiously opened a cupboard.

The lady heard that I was awake. I didn't have time to

98

hide before she came into the room. She invited me to follow her into the kitchen. She gave me a steaming plate. It was a hot soup. I didn't know what was in it, but its aroma was intoxicating. I drank it first in little sips, then gradually more greedily. The hunger that had been my constant companion in the camp returned, but in the end my stomach seemed to find some kind of satisfaction. The two women, Pani Bronisława and her mother, watched me from a few feet away. They looked contentedly at one another. I was behaving almost normally, and I seemed to be well on the way to integration now that I had consumed my first meal. Or so they thought.

The illusion didn't last for long, however. After a few hours I felt a terrible stomach ache. I couldn't stand up. I developed a fever. I turned pale and my heartbeat slowed down.

The lady was worried, and thought I was dying. She ran from the house. As quickly as she could she went and knocked at the door of the home of a doctor in the city, and begged him to come with her.

They arrived to find me almost in a coma. I had an intestinal obstruction that was getting worse and could have been fatal. And yet – I don't know how – they managed to bring down my fever. Within a few hours I was much better.

She mustn't eat like that, the doctor said to the lady, referring to me. *She needs to accustom herself gradually to food.* For now, he went on, give her nothing but goat's milk.

The goat's milk came from a place far from our home. Every day I had to walk along some streets with the lady to reach the home of a woman who raised some animals. I liked the animals. The goats were quite tame, and would actually let you stroke them. But I couldn't stand the taste of their milk. Incredibly, though, even though I felt like vomiting when I drank it, I didn't feel ill afterwards. As the days passed, I felt better. I was always given a big cup, half a litre, and every time would hope there would be a bit of foam so that there was less liquid to drink. But the lady was careful, and if she saw that there was too much foam, she would say: *a bit more milk*. Sometimes the milk became even more undrinkable. From time to time the lady added herbs of some kind which she said were special. I don't know what the herbs were. They had a bitter taste, but I had to gulp them down. I couldn't protest.

The camp left me with lots of scars. I suffered from tuberculosis, and I had problems with circulation in my legs and arms. Sometimes I became aware of my injuries. Sometimes the tattoo on my arm stung. I instinctively hid it away from everyone. I know that the lady and her mother were aware of its existence, its significance, but they didn't say anything. It was as if the camp and what had happened there were something that needed to be archived away. But its darkness, the pain it caused, had to be removed, and that was that. It wasn't a wish; it was an order. In the same way that tattoo was there, clearly visible, but it was as if it didn't exist.

And yet, everything in Oświęcim spoke of what had happened. Even the house we lived in. It had belonged to a Jewish family. The Germans gave it to the lady and her husband when they expropriated their property in Birkenau. But its walls still bore signs of the former owners. Standing proudly in the kitchen was an old menorah that the family had had to leave behind when they were moved to the Warsaw ghetto. In the past, the candles would have been lit at the beginning of Shabbat. Now it was ignored. And yet there it was, in our house, saying that the past was still present, that even those walls had a story to tell of suffering and abuse. The lady said nothing about that Jewish family: they would never be coming back. Sentence had been delivered. The house no longer belonged to them. That was what fate had decreed. Or, rather, the evil of human beings.

Our lives pass, but the places where we have lived remain. The land that the lady and her husband owned in Birkenau before the construction of the camp was still there. It had been walked for years by deportees and Germans. They drove in the rivets that held the train tracks, the sleepers that lay between the rails and kept them parallel. Many people died on that land. Hundreds of thousands of people passed through that gate without knowing that the lady who adopted me, Bronisława Rydzikowska, had lived there for a while. Without knowing that before Birkenau there had been a normal life there. A normal house, which had become the gateway to hell.

And so the walls, the ceilings, even the furniture in my new home in Oświęcim talked about the people who were no longer there. Its owners had probably been killed. The doors of the cupboards that opened and closed in peace time were still there, opened and closed by other people. Fate had made their lives cross in the most cynical and horrible way.

The last synagogue in Oświęcim, the one on Kościelny Square, is no longer the same. It too was stolen from its legitimate owners, stripped of all its assets – its books, its prayers, its rites, its incense. Some Jews who survived Birkenau and returned to the city go back there from time to time, but the ancient rites have struggled to reassert themselves. What happened in Oświęcim was too terrible for everything to resume its proper place.

The lady kept me far from the synagogue. The tattoo

on my arm made many people in the city think that I was Jewish, and she wanted to avoid that at all costs. Not because she was anti-Semitic; on the contrary: her family had been part of the anti-Nazi resistance and her brother was shot by firing squad in Auschwitz. He was arrested because he had brought assistance to the prisoners in the camp. Her parents had died shortly after their son's arrest, one from a heart attack, the other from a stroke. And she never forgot that family story; in fact, she was proud of it. Nonetheless, the fear that the enemy might return in spite of everything, or that the persecutions might in some way start all over again, was too great for everyone, including her. She feared for me. And she feared for herself.

She was the one who told me about what happened in the spring of 1941 just outside the synagogue. All the Jews of Oświęcim were gathered together and made to line up for an inspection, which was still unusual for citizens. They were counted and registered, and then they were deported somewhere else, most of them to the ghettos of Będzin, Sosnowiec and Chrzanów. They tried to make it look like the offer of a new and more comfortable place to live, but few people, if any, believed it: it was the first step of the journey to extermination.

After the liberation of Auschwitz, some of them came back. They restored the cemetery and the synagogue, and set up a house of public prayer. They wanted to come together again and start over. Very gradually, however, the community dissolved. They couldn't stay, they said. They couldn't do it. Oświęcim evoked ghosts that were still too vivid in everyone's hearts. Leaving was the only possible solution for everyone, the only way to try to start again, not to collapse beneath the weight of the terrible injustices.

In spite of all the lady's efforts, some of her acquaintances called me 'the Jewess'. *How is the little Jewess?* they would ask. So the children I had started playing with in the courtyard of the building or in the surrounding fields would repeat to me: *My mum says you're a Jew.* I tried to explain to them that I wasn't, but their conviction was unshakeable. The tattoo seemed to bear out their suspicions. It was the mark that distinguished me from the Poles and made me different. Given their insistence, I began to doubt and asked the lady if it was definitely true that I wasn't Jewish. She reminded me of my story, and also of my mother, who had been deported along with me, even if it didn't come to her entirely naturally. If she could avoid it, she didn't talk about her. I, too, was supposed to forget my mother.

At any rate, something of the culture, the spirit of the Jews who had been my companions in suffering, had

26 May 2021: Pope Francis kisses the number tattooed on Lidia's arm during her imprisonment in Birkenau concentration camp.

Lidia on the steps of the railway carriage on her arrival in Moscow.

Lidia with Aleksander Boczarow, her natural father, in the station in Moscow.

Lidia with Anna Boczarowa, her natural mother, in the Leningrad Hotel, Moscow.

Lidia with Bronisława Rydzikowska (her adoptive mother, *left*) and Anna Boczarowa (her natural mother, *right*), in the Leningrad Hotel, Moscow.

Lidia's natural family waiting for her arrival at the railway station in Moscow: her parents and the three sisters born after her mother's deportation, Olga, Rima and Swietłana.

Lidia at the age of five.

Lidia on the day of
her first communion.

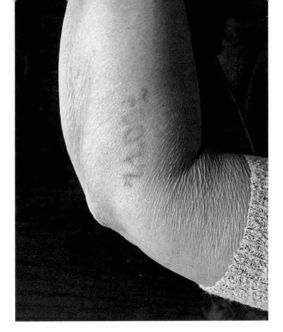

The number tattooed on Lidia's arm in Birkenau.

Lidia in front of the Gate of Death during a visit to Auschwitz.

Bronisława Rydzikowska,
Lidia's adoptive mother.

Lidia at the age of eighteen,
the first photograph sent to the
Red Cross investigation office
in Hamburg.

Lidia with her natural mother, Anna Boczarowa, and Tadeusz Szymański, the curator of Auschwitz Museum. He was responsible for the stories of the children of Auschwitz and helped Lidia to contact the office in Hamburg.

The SS Hygiene Institute with Lidia's name and number.

Lidia with the count
of the Castello di
Castellamonte,
Tomaso Ricardi di
Netro, and his assistant
Renata Rychlik.

Lidia with Evelyn
Cretier, the symbol
of her lost childhood,
during their walk
along the tracks at
Birkenau.

stayed with me; it had entered my soul. So much so that for days, once I was out of the camp, I repeated aloud the Hebrew word *Shĕmà* which, when addressed to God, means 'listen'. This word was a kind of litany recited by the children in the barrack. And I still repeat it today. It's part of me now.

One day Bronisława asked me why I still called her 'Pani'. She said that, if I wanted her to, she could simply be my new mother, or at least an aunt, so I could call her that. In retrospect, when I go back to those days, I can guess all her suffering. Pani Bronisława wanted to be my mother; she wanted it with the whole of her being. She had no children. She hadn't managed to have any. In the camp she chose one of the very smallest children there. She did it because she wanted a child all to herself, to fill the gap that the lack of children had left inside her. And yet, I'm sure, she also did it out of love. Out of the need for love. And in some way, even though she was a stiff and strict woman, that love reached me.

It was very difficult for me to adapt to normal life. For one, I wouldn't stop moving about. After all the days I had spent rocking back and forth in the barrack at the camp, it didn't seem possible to me that I was finally able to go outside and run and jump among the meadows. For the first few days I wanted to put on the shoes, both left feet, that I wore when I left the camp. And also a huge red jumper that was tied behind my back when I left. I don't remember where I'd found those things, but I'd got used to them. Pani Bronisława intervened, however, and threw everything away. It was a little trauma for me. At first I resolved it by walking around barefoot. It would be some time before I wore normal shoes, right and left, like all the other children.

The worst suffering was at the table. Once I had recovered from that initial indigestion, I could eat everything. I was able to do it with my hands, although I could only eat greedily. As soon as some food was set down in front of me on a plate, I devoured it one mouthful after another. I didn't chew very much, gulping down the food almost whole. That speed was also the product of the fear I had experienced in the camp – that other children might steal the food that I was given, or that the Germans might take it away from me out of spite. We had to feed ourselves quickly, and no delays were permitted. So much so that even today, many years later, I still tend to eat that way. It's at the end of every meal, however, that I do the worst violence to myself. I have to force myself not to hide a piece of food in my napkin and take it away. The temptation is enormous; I still feel it in restaurants and have to tell myself not to do it. The experience of the camp was so over-whelming; the urge to survive so powerful in the face of everyone and everything. That sense of an imminent ending turned me, turned all of us, into predators.

There are so many things that I struggled to do immediately after leaving Birkenau. Among those things was climbing stairs. I didn't know how to, and I was frightened of them. When I found myself close to them I would start crawling. Pani Bronisława wasn't very patient; she often got angry. But sometimes she understood that she had to give in, she had to surrender. Taking the upper hand wasn't always the right strategy with me. She soon worked it out: if she let me vent my fury, I would eventually get tired, become more docile and tend to obey her.

After a few weeks I gave in. *If you really don't want to call me Mama, at least call me Aunt*, she said again. It seemed to be a good compromise. And so she became my aunt, and became closer to me than she had been until then. And shortly after that she became Mama, Mama Bronisława. Admittedly she was still bossy, but I gained a certain confidence with her. In fact, it didn't take me long to understand that for good or ill this was my new family and she was my adoptive mother, the woman I was destined to grow up with.

With the passing of time, the restlessness that was so typical of me when I had just left the camp began to subside. I got used to my new routine even though I went on living as if the camp had never entirely left me: I obeyed Mama Bronisława without showing her all of my feelings, often in silence. The survival tactic that I learned in Birkenau was still my way of facing the world. One example of this is something that happened one cold winter morning.

It was a clear day, but the streets were entirely covered with snow. Mama Bronisława decided to take me out for a walk. I always loved the open air; I didn't like playing at home. I irritably threw away a little doll that I'd been given as a present. I didn't like classic children's games; my only amusement was running in the fields, taking deep breaths of the clean air, enjoying the freedom that the camp had denied me. So Mama Bronisława tied a rope to a sled and pulled me through the streets of the city. Also with me on the sled was a baby goat that I usually played with in the courtyard at home. I held it between my legs and stroked it. We didn't weigh very much, and transporting us wasn't a huge effort. Eventually Mama Bronisława heard a bleating sound, so she stopped and looked around and saw there was nobody on the sled that she was pulling. The little kid and I had fallen off. The animal was complaining while I sat on the ground, covered with snow, but didn't cry or protest. If the baby goat hadn't been there, Mama Bronisława might not have noticed that she'd lost me. I had been taught to remain silent and not complain, so that was what I did. Mama Bronisława hugged me and asked me why I never cried. I looked at her without replying, but let her stroke my hair and rest my head against her chest. I was hard to get through to; deep inside myself, more than living, I was still just surviving. And I was convinced that sooner or later Anna, my real mother, would come back to me and everything would start all over again like before, when we were together in the woods of Belarus.

In any case, I learned to love Mama Bronisława, who, even though she was bossy, did everything she could to make me feel at ease. And I also tried to love her husband, who had by now returned safe and sound from the German camps. Mama Bronisława was a meticulous woman, a perfectionist. She always tried to dress me very carefully, and made my clothes and skirts herself. She wanted to present me to the whole of Oświęcim in a particular way – nicely combed; she wanted people to compliment her on my prettiness. At home she had a newspaper cutting with a photograph of Shirley Temple, the girl with the golden curls. That was her model. She wanted me to dance with her but she never managed to persuade me. My ringlets were the same as hers, however. When we went out she would introduce me to her friends as her little Shirley Temple. I wasn't interested in those things, but I went along with it. I smiled as best I could. And I accepted her friends' compliments without comment.

I was very good with the other children, and was particularly good at hide and seek. The camp had been a great teacher in that respect. It was there that I had learned how to disappear from everyone, to slip inside the most unthinkable nooks and crannies, make myself invisible, spend whole hours without making a sound. I also noticed that cats, when they are scared, escape to inaccessible places. And from there they observe what's happening outside without being seen. So I did the same thing. Basically playing hide and seek was finding places where I felt safe and from which I could observe what was happening without anyone knowing where I was.

One day I decided to hide in a gap among the bushes just outside the courtyard of the house. I went inside cautiously, taking care not to leave any traces behind me. The other children started looking for me but couldn't find me. After a while they got bored and stopped looking.

But I didn't come out. I stayed there, shut away in my hiding place. I had no intention of coming out. I thought again of the times in the barrack when Dr Mengele came to get us. I would creep under the wooden shelves, all the way to the wall. It was impossible for them to see me. I closed my eyes and spoke in silence to my mother. *They won't get me*, I said to her. *I will resist for you.* In the little opening in the bushes I shut my eyes and talked to her again. *You can't be dead*, I said to her. *One day you'll find me and we'll be together again.*

Towards evening I heard Mama Bronisława calling me. She was worried. She hadn't seen me all afternoon. No one knew where I was. Then I decided to come out. I walked towards her and she hugged me. I said: *You don't need to be so worried about me. I was just playing hide and seek.*

At kindergarten I was very restless and couldn't sit still. Eventually the staff gave in and left me free to roam around as I wanted because it was impossible to keep me busy with any other activity. After kindergarten I started primary school. For that I had to be recorded in the civil registry. At the same time Mama Bronisława decided that I needed to be christened. If I put some clues together in retrospect, I deduce that she must have known much more about me than I thought she did. That my mother was Catholic, for example, and so was my whole birth family.

At any rate, she told the priest in Oświęcim that I had been born into a Catholic family so I needed to receive the sacrament. She too was a devout believer, as was her husband – or at least that was what they said. Their religiosity had a strictness to it that made them severe, people with solid moral principles. I don't remember the day of the christening, but I came out of it with a new name, the name under which I'm still recorded in the state registry: Lidia. From that day that's what I've officially called myself. And for the whole of Oświęcim I became 'Lidia from the camp'. I didn't rebel against that change. It was what my adoptive mother had decided, and I went along with it. Basically, I thought, Luda to Lidia wasn't a huge change. In fact, with the christening I really became her daughter. I had a first name that I didn't have before, and I had a surname that wasn't mine. I was Polish; my Russian roots no longer existed. In those times, still shaken by a war that had destroyed archives and families, that was how it worked; there were no alternatives. And besides, no one had come looking for me. No one had put in any request about me. There was no sign, no word of my real family. As far as the whole of Oświęcim was concerned, my parents had disappeared. All that remained was for me to integrate into that community.

And yet the past, not just my mother, was still very

much alive within me. They soon realized this at school. One day at playtime I decided to take charge of the games. I called all the children to gather round me. The teachers weren't keeping an eye on us at that moment; they were talking among themselves without paying us much attention.

Schnell! Quickly!

The order had come out of my mouth before I was really aware of it.

Schnell!

Just like that, the order from the SS when they had to line us up outside the barrack to choose who was going with Mengele, or when they rounded up all the deportees who had just arrived at the camp to decide who was going to the gas chamber and who could consider themselves safe, at least for now.

My classmates joined in with the game. They didn't know what the word meant. They didn't know what I was doing, but they obeyed. They stood in line, side by side, while I, with a stick wedged under my armpit as if it were an SS man's whip, inspected everyone with a grim and inquisitorial expression. I studied them one by one, lifting their faces with the stick by putting it under their chins. I asked their names, how old they were, where they came from. I explained that they mustn't breathe, because any

113

false move could have fatal consequences. Since they had behaved badly, half of them were going to end up in the gas ovens. *You don't see the smoke coming from the chimney over there?* I ask. *That's where half of you are going to end up. And then your bodies will be burnt. There'll be nothing left of you. Just ash and dust like what's under your feet right now.* Some of them laugh; some don't. So I make my decision. Certain of them have to take a step towards me. They are the ones who will die.

What's going on here? The voice of the teacher behind me is alarmed. I turn around and see that she and her colleagues are studying me with horror. They immediately suspend the game and take me aside. They ask me what on earth I am up to. They call Mama Bronisława. They tell her everything and she comes and takes me home. The other children tell their parents about the game and all hell breaks loose. They think I'm dangerous, that I might teach their children to become murderers.

Mama Bronisława was furious: *What on earth was I playing at?* she asked me. Then I was punished by being forbidden to leave the house for a few days. *What you saw in the camp no longer exists*, she said to me.

As always, I accepted her decisions, her punishment. But in terms of setting an example, she didn't touch me. I wasn't afraid of anything. I was Lidia from the camp.

I'd been through hell. I'd come out alive. *Schnell! Schnell!* All day, the cry of the Germans echoed within me. I would come to realize that it had been impressed upon me more than I wanted to know. That didn't mean that I, a victim, had become a perpetrator. That would have been impossible. But the words of the perpetrators had become something like a second skin. Whether I wanted it or not, they were part of me.

There was one thing that I hadn't brought with me from the camp: selfishness. The teachers noticed. My adoptive mother still sent me to school with a roll. Unlike when I was in the camp and gulped down the little food that I could find without sharing it, here, on the contrary, I shared it with any of my companions who wanted some. I discovered the joy of sharing – something that I'd never felt before. Perhaps it was a lesson that my real mother had taught me without meaning to. If she found food, she always brought it to me; she gave up her own food to let me have some. That was clearly her legacy, and it came out at school. Mama Bronisława was happy about that, even if she said to me: *Make sure you have enough for yourself.*

In the mornings of the cold season I was often late for school. Winters in Poland can be tough. A lot of snow falls. And for me the call of the snow was irresistible.

Before going to class I would run to the top of a little hill near the school. My satchel became a sled. I would slide down to the bottom of the hill several times. Often I was drenched by the time I got to school. Luckily the teachers, strict though they were, knew what the extermination camps had been like, and knew about my story in there. Then they tried to be indulgent with me. They undressed me and put my clothes to dry on a big stove. They accepted my liveliness and did their best to live with it. Mama Bronisława did the same.

I was happy that I had a mother like everyone else. When I was with my classmates I did call her 'Mama'. And I called her husband 'Papa'. Basically I was at ease with him too. The best thing was when he put me on his back and we left the house together. We would walk towards the river. The water was clean. There were lots of fish. We threw fishing lines at the end of rods. Such excitement when the little floats disappeared into the water, such excitement bringing fish to the riverbank. Those were carefree days that helped me feel as if I was part of a family. I would never forget my real mother Anna, my father Aleksander, my grandparents, my brother Michał. But over time their faces blurred, and my longing for them became less and less urgent.

There were also other children on the river with us, and

we spent whole days in the open air. Soon Oświęcim became a friendly place. Soon it became my home. Sometimes Mama Bronisława would make clothes for the other children too, giving them as presents. When she did that I realized I was jealous.

Life in Oświęcim after the war had to take into account the awkward presence of the two extermination camps: Auschwitz on one side, Birkenau not far away on the other. 'My' camp, Birkenau, was left there after the liberation, with its fate in the balance. No one knew exactly what to do with it. The gates were open. No one guarded it. There was as yet no need to remember, or to keep the evidence of what had happened as a warning. The evil was too close to be digested, or for us to talk about it. And yet the camp was still standing. There were its barracks, the barbed wire all around, the ruins of the gas ovens. There was the entrance tower from which the SS watched over the convoys. There were the tracks beside which the deportees were divided into two lines – one for death, one for life. Now they were empty and silent, like the traces of the paths and roads taken by the SS and the inmates. The panorama, apart from the ruins of the ovens, was still the same. Trees and meadows separated the fence from the Vistula, the river all the inmates dreamed of reaching. It meant freedom, flight from the Germans. It was all still there, a monster emptied of its soul.

My uncle, Mama Bronisława's brother, had a plot of land bordering Birkenau, where he had built a cottage. Every now and again I would go and see him with other children. It just took a moment to climb the fence and get into the camp. The first few times I was hesitant. In the distance I could see my barrack, the place where I had suffered for so many months. I was attracted, but also frightened. Until one day some other children called to me from inside. *Lidia, are you not coming?* They seemed to know the place well. In fact, I would discover that I was perhaps the only child in Oświęcim who hadn't set foot in it after the liberation. For the other children the camp was a place like many others where you could play hide and seek undisturbed. The adults, for their part, had long ago taken away everything they could find from the place, without respect for what had happened there.

I climbed over the fence and got in. They asked me to play with them. The call was irresistible. Once again, the camp became a familiar place for me as well. I wandered the length and breadth of it. I went into different barracks, including mine. I touched the drawings left on the walls by the children. I ran in the corridors and jumped on the shelves where I had once been able to do nothing but sit and rock back and forth. The emotion soon faded, and the barracks stopped scaring me. I especially liked climbing up to the towers and looking down on the camp as the Germans had done.

The other children and I divided up the camp to play hide and seek. Here too I always won. I'm good at hiding where no one would think of looking for me. I hid for months in there, and I still do it today. I could see the path that my mother crept along to get to my barrack. I thought I could see her, young Anna who had done so much to keep me alive beside her. Every now and again I would go all the way to where the ovens had been. And along the tracks where I last saw my grandparents and Michał. But then I would immediately start playing again. I had no more tears. I just wanted to live.

Of course, I remembered the cold of those winter months. Now it was summer, and grass and wildflowers were growing around the barracks. Sun warmed the earth. So much light seemed impossible, such an explosion of life. Most people seemed to have been utterly indifferent to what went on in there. Where once there had been the stench of burning flesh, nature had taken back its spaces and was now their uncontested ruler. I acted as a guide for some of the children. I told them who had been in the barracks, what the watchtowers were for, and the big tower by the entrance, the tracks with the goods wagons coming into the camp. I told them what it had been like. I talked to them about it as a child can talk about such things. Simply, but also truthfully. Children don't know how to make things up. They talk about what they know, what they've seen, what they've experienced.

And perhaps that's why even today, when I'm asked if it's right to bring children to visit Birkenau and the other extermination and concentration camps, I say yes. I know that most parents prefer to bring them only once they're grown up, and I respect that choice. But at the same time I don't think it does the younger ones any harm to see how things were. In fact, it might help them to understand how far into the abyss man can plunge. To what level of cruelty. I've seen children like them in there. They've looked evil in the face; they've had to come to terms with it. Today there's nothing to fear for them, but everyone has a duty to remember. To know and understand this could be crucial for future generations. I don't believe that the plague of anti-Semitism has died out. Even today its seeds are still alive in our Europe. If we are to make sure that that horror is never repeated, we need men and women who have developed a critical consciousness, who are able to rebel against those who foment hatred and division. Who can say yes to an acceptance of all kinds of diversity, who know that they are people of love and life. To shape citizens like that you need to act when they are still children. Not just tell, but also show. A visit to Birkenau in someone's youth can become a fixed point in their lives, evidence that they will never be able to forget. That's how I see it.

I was recently struck by the words of the Jewish writer Edith Bruck. She says that years after her deportation she came back to her village in Hungary. It was some time in the 1980s. She was invited to visit a school. All the children were wearing a red ribbon, because the Communist Party was still in power. She read out an extract from her book dedicated to the Shoah, then asked the class: *What do you know about the history of the village?* A girl stood up and replied: *There was a very rich Jewish woman who lived near the cemetery. One day some people* – the girl couldn't say who they were – *came and told her to leave.* Bruck said in an interview:

That was what they taught the children. Nothing. They didn't know that we were deported, persecuted. That the people who came to take us were Germans and that the intention of those Germans was to exterminate us. We can't be surprised that Jews are insulted in the street in Hungary today. That these horrible stories have returned. About rich Jews, about Jews controlling the world. That there's this ferocious anti-Semitism. I wrote this book because I believe it's much more important to remember today than it was sixty years ago. A black cloud is falling over Europe once again.

When I was exploring the camp, I discovered that many of the barracks of Birkenau no longer existed, and had been demolished. They were, in fact, used to build most of the little houses that were now going up around the camp, including the one that belonged to my uncle. The Poles resumed what the Germans had done back then, when they expropriated and demolished their dwellings to build the barracks for the deportees. Luckily not everything was taken away from the camp, and most of the structures were left standing. My barrack, for example: I found the drawings done on the central wall, I believe by some Jewish deportees who arrived from Warsaw in the final months leading up to the liberation. I found again that smell of mustiness and death. I found the signs of a life in captivity that would remain for ever the darkest part of my existence.

The 1950s in Oświęcim were simple and beautiful. There were no cars in the city. There was a great deal of poverty, but no one was sad. Every now and again my baptismal godmother would come to see me from Krakow, always driven by her husband. When she arrived, the whole of Oświęcim would assemble to look at this vehicle, which evoked dreams and impossible flight.

Everyone walked everywhere. Some rode on bicycles. If several people had to move together, they would use horse-drawn carts. Women spent many hours in the laundry washing clothes. Here they would talk for ages about everything and everyone, swapping confidences. Many of the men worked in the little factories in the area, and spent almost all their free time playing cards or sitting outside their front doors talking to anyone who passed. Very few travelled outside of Oświęcim, and no one of my acquaintance ever crossed the borders of Poland. The children made up all kinds of games. Nature was our friend, and it helped us: we climbed on the trees, we waded in the streams, ran in the fields, chased after hares and pheasants. Our favourite game consisted of coming down the hills using sacks as sleds, both on grass in summer and on snow in winter. Or, with a length of elastic in our hands, we would play at creating new shapes and passing the elastic from hand to hand. When we had nothing to play with, we would simply enjoy running after one another.

On Friday evening everyone went to church for communal prayer. There were two churches in Oświęcim, one in the main square, the other more hidden away and devoted to the Salesian community. On Saturday we would polish our shoes for Sunday mass, in which the whole village participated – the women in the pews, the men mostly outside in the churchyard. Mama Bronisława tried to dress me as best she could. When the bishop came they would choose me, along with another girl, to welcome him, carrying flowers, on the steps at the entrance to the church. Mama Bronisława looked at me with pride: her little princess.

These were days of great solidarity. There wasn't much wealth around, and the consequences of the war were still clearly apparent. But everyone shared the little they had – flour, sugar, the occasional egg. There was an enchantment about that time that cannot be fully conveyed.

Since my adoptive parents were very religious, in the morning we prayed together at the breakfast table, and in the evening the praying was done on our knees in front of an image of the Madonna. I grew up in the Catholic faith as they wished, but in the awareness that the belief was the same as that of my real parents.

I have never interpreted Catholicism as meaning that one belongs to a community that is somehow separate or better. For me it was always an opportunity to learn the opposite of the ideology of the camp: sharing, love of the last, the Gospel of the Beatitudes according to which we are all equal in the eyes of God. This is my faith and even today I want to testify to it by relating its opposite: the Nazi horror and its homicidal rage.

Among the many children I played with there was one I was particularly fond of, and with whom I got on very well. Her name was Lusia. She was Jewish, but no one knew much more about her origins. She had been with me in the camp; we knew each other from Birkenau. I remember her on the shelves, rocking back and forth, resisting as I did. She too was adopted by a family that lived near our house. We spent many afternoons together, and were the same age. One afternoon after school I went down into the courtyard thinking that I would find her there as ever. And she was there, but she wasn't alone. She was sitting on the knee of a young woman I had never seen before. The woman was stroking her hair. Lusia gave a slightly embarrassed smile. I stood frozen for several minutes. I couldn't take my eyes off the scene.

I understood that this woman was Lusia's biological mother. She had looked for her and found her. Who knows what far-away country she had come from. And yet she had done it. She had crossed borders, overcome obstacles and difficulties, but she had found her daughter again.

That embrace between them opened up a gap within me that I couldn't entirely decipher. I started crying without knowing exactly why. And suddenly I wondered aloud: *How come my mother didn't come and get me?*

I asked Mama Bronisława for an explanation: why had my mother Anna not come looking for me? And I used some cruel words, the words of a wounded child: *You're very ugly, but my real mother was beautiful and had long hair; she wasn't like you at all.*

Mama Bronisława wept. She told me I was a bad, ungrateful child, and she told me to put my heart at peace: *Unfortunately your mother is no longer in this world!*

In fact, it wasn't true that I was ungrateful, but the separation from my mother was not a wound that could be easily healed. She still lived within me. And there was something else. However much they told me that she was dead, I was convinced of the opposite. Before leaving the camp I didn't see her corpse. There was a pile of bodies heaped up outside the children's barrack, but I couldn't remember recognizing her. Of course, it was impossible to recognize all the faces in that horrible tangle, and yet there was a vivid sense in my mind that she had made it out alive, that she had left Birkenau on one of the last marches led by the Germans. That I was told she was dead because no one knew what to say to me. And that now she was alive. I just didn't understand why she hadn't come to get me.

As time passed, Mama Anna was mentioned less and less. But I guessed from little signs that the idea that she was dead was a wish of Mama Bronisława and not a demonstrated truth. All in all I understood that if she was alive, I would have to do something to find her. But it wasn't easy.

From time to time the radio was turned on at home, and one day I listened to a programme in which they broadcast the appeals of some families looking for their own loved ones who had disappeared after the Shoah. They thought they might still be alive somewhere in the world and wanted to find them again. Would the voice of Mama Anna be among them one day? I couldn't help wondering. I turned on the radio more and more often, in the hope something so devoutly wished for might become reality.

One day, when I was perhaps ten or eleven, there was a knock at the door. Mama Bronisława opened it. It was a neighbour who started talking in a low voice. I tried to get closer unnoticed. I made out some words that took my breath away: on the radio, the neighbour said, I thought I heard that someone was looking for your Lidia. Mama Bronisława didn't reply; she just gestured to her to be quiet, not to say anything, and sent her away.

Now I knew the truth. Someone was looking for me. I wasn't sure that it was Mama Anna, but at any rate there was someone who was asking for me. And yet my life continued as before. Today, looking back, I don't hold anything against Mama Bronisława, and in some ways I can excuse her: she was afraid of losing me. But in those days I thought only of how I could be reunited with whoever it was who was looking for me. I had to be careful, I had to put out feelers, because sooner or later they would find me, I thought. At home I maintained the attitude of respect and submission that I had always shown. Except that every now and again I would come out with some poisonous comment. Usually it was the one directed at Mama Bronisława: *You're ugly, and my mother was beautiful.*

Months passed, then years. By now I was about thirteen. I helped at home, I lent a hand with the cleaning. I was fluent in Polish, and felt Polish as well. I had heard nothing more about my mother Anna. Sometimes I convinced myself that they weren't talking about me in that radio broadcast. Perhaps they were looking for another little girl, and our neighbour had made a mistake. One day when I went into Mama Bronisława's room to tidy it, in an open drawer I saw an envelope among the bedsheets. I took it without thinking too much about it. It was open, and bore the insignia of the International Red Cross. Inside there was a letter, bearing the same letterhead. A few lines stopped my heart: they were asking whether there was a little girl by the name of Lyudmila Boczarowa in the house. Lyudmila, my Russian name. Boczarow, the surname of my biological parents. It didn't say that Mama Anna was alive, or that my father Aleksander was either. The letter contained nothing more. It was impossible to tell who exactly was looking for me, but somebody was. And that was enough for me.

I quickly put the letter back. I left the room and when Mama Bronisława came back I didn't mention what I had seen. I decided to keep it to myself. I was worried that she might get angry, and I didn't feel like arguing. It was enough for me to know that someone was looking for me, enough for me to hope that perhaps my mother Anna was alive. In bed at night I closed my eyes and thought about her. And I dreamed of the day when I might hug her once again. It had to happen sooner or later. I was only fourteen, and in spite of all the experiences I had had in the past, I didn't have the strength to do anything but dream. And I wouldn't forget that I owed a debt of respect and gratitude to Mama

Bronisława, that she gave me a home after the camp. I had been very lucky to end up where I did. Oświęcim was now my family. If I left, I didn't know where I would go. In Belarus we had lived in the woods. And besides, if my mother was alive, where was she? I was told at school that Belarus was now part of the Soviet Union and was ruled by Stalin. The countries under Russian rule included Poland, which had moved in a few years from Nazi to Communist control. All the countries behind that Iron Curtain were not free. We were not free. If my mother was alive, I thought, finding me under these conditions was an impossible undertaking. Perhaps that was why the Red Cross had become involved. Perhaps that was why she had approached a non-partisan international organization. I was beginning to understand the world I lived in, the nature of my situation. I started doing some research and my own political situation came slowly into focus.

Eventually some of my schoolmates started helping me. I was no longer a child, and they were the ones who were surprised that I wasn't looking for my mother. They knew I was Lidia from the camp. They knew my story, and they knew that Mama Bronisława wasn't my biological mother. *Why don't you do something about it?* they asked. And to spur me on, they gave me some addresses of search centres in cities around Poland. Those were places you could go to, leave your own name and see if in other parts of the country, or even in other countries, someone was looking for you in another office. I decided to act without telling Mama Bronisława. I didn't want to frighten her; I didn't want her to think I wished to leave. Not least because that wasn't my intention. I just wanted to know what had happened to Mama Anna, that was all. And if she was alive, I wanted to hug her again.

In the search office at Krakow, the biggest city near Oświęcim, they suggested that I try writing to the International Red Cross which was based in Hamburg. The Red Cross again. It looked as if I was on the right path. I gave my address for any replies as the search office. Some months passed and out of the blue an initial reply arrived. It was a telegram, saying simply that they were going to put out a search for me. My heart leapt. There was someone in Germany who was willing to do something for a stranger, for a Belarussian girl abandoned in Poland.

For many years I lived with the suspicion that my mother wasn't dead. Now I had a way of checking. Mama Bronisława, however, wasn't naive. She could read between the lines and guessed things I thought she couldn't have known. She knew I was up to something, and it wasn't hard for her to check. One day she confronted me straight up: *I know what you're doing*, she said.

How can you? I replied.

I know, and that's it. Then she asked me: *Does it mean you want to leave me?*

I said: *No. It means I want to know the truth.*

We fell silent. We didn't know what else to say. Then she broke the ice: *Why didn't you say anything to me? There was so much I could have told you. And everything would have been much simpler, particularly now that I know you don't want to leave me.*

We hugged and I felt relieved. She had found me out, but accepted what was happening. I hadn't lied to her. I wanted with all my heart to hug my mother again, or at least know what had happened to her, but at the same time I felt that I didn't want to flee Poland, that the camp and Oświęcim had mysteriously taken hold of me. I thought that Mama Bronisława must have kept something about Mama Anna hidden from me, the news from the radio, the letter among the bedlinen, simply out of fear of losing me. Not to stop me from trying to find out the truth. For years she was only terrified of the possibility of being left on her own again.

Now she started helping me with the Red Cross. She had come over to my side. She helped me when they asked to photograph the shape of my skull and one of my ears, and to send them blood samples. In Hamburg they wanted to do things properly; they didn't want to make mistakes.

Some months passed. I was starting to give up hope because the wait seemed too long. But just as I was thinking that everything was lost, a letter arrived for me from Hamburg. The Red Cross told me first of all that there was no trace of my brother Michał. All information about him, unfortunately, stopped in Birkenau. And then they wrote these words, which took my breath away: 'It is not as you think, your mother is not dead. She lives in the Soviet Union. She too has been looking desperately for you for years, and by way of identification please tell her where possible the number of the tattoo that you were given on your arm.'

It seems that in the special archives they had found the information about the transport of my mother Anna from Auschwitz to Bergen-Belsen, and the unexpected liberation that followed. Then they looked for her, again via the Red Cross in Russia, and found her.

I didn't know what to say. I had conflicted emotions. In spite of what I read in the letter I couldn't help wondering why, if she really was alive, she hadn't done everything she could to find me. Perhaps she didn't need me. Perhaps she didn't love me as I loved her.

6

L IVING IN POLAND AFTER THE LIBERATION wasn't easy. But it only dawned on me once I was an adult that this was also the case in many of the neighbouring countries, including the Soviet Union.

The great terror of the war didn't end in 1945. Unfortunately it had a long way to go. The German defeat didn't open up scenarios of paradise on earth but, at least for one part of Europe, horizons of darkness and suffering. The heart of all of this was Central Europe, and with it the Soviet Union. The Red Army had liberated the German camps, but it also meant that many Poles were forced to return home, unable to move or travel. In many cases those who rebelled against the new regime were deported to other concentration camps, the Soviet gulags. They too were places of death and despair. A certain amount of oppression was part of everyday life. The Communist regimes of the countries around the Soviet Union owed it respect and obedience. After the shadow of Hitler, the shadow of Stalin, of Moscow, fell upon that part of Europe. Poland, Czechoslovakia, Hungary, Romania and Bulgaria fell into a new nightmare.

The largest apartments in Moscow and St Petersburg were turned into communal apartments, and similar things happened to the apartments in other Soviet cities. Once again, as in Oświęcim before the camp was built in Birkenau, many houses were expropriated. In the Soviet Union, however, they weren't destroyed but reused. They were called *kommunalka* – apartments designed to optimise the availability of living spaces. The former owners were left only one room for their families and their belongings. All the rest was assigned to strangers. Toilets and the kitchen were communal. The Soviet ideology transformed the everyday life of an entire generation. Day by day, poverty and misery became part of many people's lives.

The regime abhorred any manifestation of luxury. No affluence could be permitted. The boom beginning on the other side of the Iron Curtain, in Western Europe, was seen here as absolute evil. In fact, people wanted to climb the social ladder and attain a different lifestyle. But the regime blocked all initiatives. There was no room for dreams in this part of the world. Often there were even food shortages. For anyone who had experienced the hardships of the extermination camps, life in the Soviet Union and its satellites seemed like a cruel joke, even though nothing, obviously, was comparable to the German camps.

When my mother went back to the Soviet Union, she was in a terrible state. She was 5 ft 8 (1.74 m) and weighed barely 6 stone (37 kg). And yet – I would find out later – after a few weeks of intensive medical treatment, she decided to leave for Oświęcim in the hope of finding me. She was informed by the Red Army, however, that all the children in Birkenau had been sent to orphanages in the Soviet Union. Back at home, she was miraculously reunited with my father. Like many couples, they had agreed that if they survived the war, they would meet up in Minsk, below a monument, at a certain time of day. And that was where they found one another. Together they began to look for me in all the orphanages in the country. Their searches were in vain, however. Discouraged, they decided to leave for Donetsk, where they found refuge in the home of my father's parents. Their suffering didn't end there. The Soviet regime suspected my mother of being a Nazi spy because they thought it was impossible for anyone to have survived the camp. But she wouldn't let go. She questioned their theory and went on looking for me. She wrote some letters to the Red Cross and the Red Crescent in Moscow asking for any news of me. The only identifying mark she had was the number tattooed on me in the camp: 70072. But for years she received no news.

The first telegram from my mother reached me when I was nineteen. She asked me where I was and who was taking care of me. It was a telegram of few words, and left me dumbfounded. I would have expected a long letter, with explanations. And, in fact, there was nothing. Just two simple requests for information.

The answers were easy to give, but at first I didn't know exactly what to say. I wasn't sure that the person at the other end was the Mama Anna who brought me up in Belarus and protected me in Birkenau. I wondered: did she really search for me with such commitment? When I looked for her I managed to find her, after all. I managed to get the Red Cross to find out definite information about her. And, meanwhile, what had she done? Why had she never come back to Poland? Why hadn't she moved heaven and earth to find out what had happened to me? Why those years of silence?

I was plagued by doubts and felt a certain degree of

resentment. Mama Bronisława had brought me up; she loved me. Why, in spite of the difficulties involved in crossing borders, had Mama Anna not tried to come at least once to Birkenau? She must have known that the camp had been liberated. She was aware that many of those left behind had survived. So why didn't she move? What had stopped her from doing anything? My friends in Oświęcim encouraged me to look on the bright side. *You've found your mother*, they said to me. *You must be happy about that.* And they tried to keep my morale up.

In fact, I was in pieces. I felt betrayed. In Birkenau, Mama Anna had done everything in her power to keep me alive, but then, once the war was over, she had stayed far away. Why? Could a mother forget her daughter?

Mama Bronisława wasn't entirely at ease either. But she was more worried about me than she was about Mama Anna. She knew that the threat she had tried to defend herself against for years was now real: my natural mother could take me away. She had the right, after all. There was only one step to prevent all of this from legally happening: to marry me off to a Polish citizen before I set foot in the Soviet Union.

Arthur Maksymowicz was the same age as me. He was a neighbour, and his mother was a friend of Mama Bronisława. It was the two women who had decided

141

between them that Arthur would be the perfect person to help me with my maths studies. It was a subject that I was finding difficult, he was doing well at school, and he was able to help me with my revision.

He was a nice young man, and pleasant to be around, and we continued to see each other after leaving school. I guessed that he liked me, but at first I don't think he had any intention of getting engaged to me. I imagine that those were our mothers' plans. When I realized that, I didn't react. I accepted that things went as they wanted them to.

What else could I do? In Oświęcim, as in the rest of Poland, there were many arranged marriages. It was a practice accepted by many, not least by me.

The wedding happened shortly afterwards. It had to be organized in a hurry. Mama Anna was getting closer and closer. Even though travelling was difficult on the eastern side of the Iron Curtain, our reunion seemed imminent. And she could demand that I leave Poland.

I don't remember very much about the weeks of our engagement, but Arthur and I didn't socialise. Not a caress, not a kiss, not a conversation to give me an idea of the feelings of the man I was about to marry. It's a horrible thing to say but it's true: I wasn't in love. And yet he, Arthur, was the man I was destined to spend the rest of my life with. How could I possibly go to the altar without being afraid, without rebelling? Well, I appealed to my own inner strength. It's hard to explain, but at that time a girl like me, taken from Birkenau and saved, could not rebel. I couldn't ask, demand, complain. I just had to obey. And I obeyed, even though I knew full well that Arthur could not bring me happiness. He could be a good husband – and, in fact, he would be – but marriage to him could not lead to my happiness, to my fulfilment. This wasn't resignation on my part; it was simply realism. And from that moment onwards I was Lidia Maksymowicz.

I was twenty-one years old, in December 1961, New Year's Eve, when we held our marriage ceremony. It was a cold day, like many I experienced in the camp when I was very young. Snow lined the streets. I felt plump and a bit clumsy in my white dress. Everyone said I looked beautiful. And, in fact, I was – at least, that was how I saw myself. I looked like my mother Anna. Mama Bronisława was radiant. Ryszard, my adoptive father, walked me to the altar in the only smart suit he owned. I said 'I do' in front of a priest and to Arthur. I was Lidia from the camp. I had been through hell. How could I ever have agreed to an arranged marriage?

The first months passed quickly, and happily, all in all. We went to live in an apartment of our own, not far from the home of my adoptive parents. Spring arrived and, in

143

April, the Red Cross told me that my mother was waiting for me in Moscow, for a meeting that the whole of the Soviet media had begun to say was historic. Yes – because all the papers, the radio and TV were talking about me. For the regime it was an opportunity to show how the Soviet Union was devoted to its scattered children, and wanted them back under its wing.

Rumours also began circulating here in Poland about the imminent meeting. All of a sudden I found myself at the centre of an unimaginable media frenzy. It was as if two big countries, Poland and the Soviet Union, were doing nothing but talk about me.

I was prepared for a meeting that seemed to be riddled with uncertainties. Even if the Red Cross maintained that my mother had been looking for me for some time, I was nervous. Apart from the doubts about the silence of all those years, there were also the doubts about the turn that my life was about to take from now on. Certainly, after my marriage – to which my adoptive mother had pushed me, but which I had accepted without demur – no one could keep me in the Soviet Union. And probably the reason I agreed to get married had been because, unconsciously, I felt that Poland was my home. I also wondered: what was I supposed to do in Donetsk? What life could I ever begin in the cold and distant Soviet Union?

The day of the meeting approached. I arrived in Moscow by train, accompanied by Mama Bronisława and Papa Ryszard. They too were agitated. The journey took for ever. We travelled in silence. We couldn't find any words to say to each other.

My heart was racing. In my mind there was a clear memory of Mama Anna's eyes. But what would her face look like today? I had been a child in Birkenau, and I was a woman in Moscow. I was here with my adoptive parents, with my husband, and with a wedding ring on my finger that said I was a Pole and planned to stay in Poland.

The train puffed as it entered Moscow station. I imagined an intimate encounter, with not many people and time and space for me and her, but when the doors of the carriage opened on to the platform, something happened that I would never have imagined: dozens of flashes went off, lighting up my face. I was Lidia from the camp, Mama Anna's Luda, and it seemed to me that the whole of the Soviet Union wanted to see what had become of me, and more particularly wanted to immortalize the hug that my mother was about to give me.

The platform was crammed with people. I didn't know anyone. The regime wanted the day to be historic: not only the Soviet Union but also the West was to know of its magnanimity. A government that was considered

145

despotic and totalitarian loved its children and wanted them to be happy, for their tears to turn to smiles, for the weeping to make way for joy.

The tension was too much for Mama Anna. It was as if she had convinced herself that the person who was about to step off the train was the Luda she had left behind in the camp, the little girl she thought she had lost for ever, the child – historians would say – who spent more time than anyone else in Birkenau. So she fainted, even before she had the chance to meet my eyes. Orderlies came running around her. I climbed down the steps of the train and only managed to glimpse a woman being taken away on a stretcher. My father alone came towards me. He was weeping, and emotional. The people around us wore heavy coats and had scarves around their necks. The women wore scarves wrapped around their heads. The sun was shining, but Moscow spring was struggling to break away from winter.

The photographers went on clicking away, and some journalists tried to extract a statement from me. My Russian was still good, but I had trouble assembling meaningful sentences. My adoptive parents shielded me, along with government representatives, although it was difficult for them to drag me away. The media were very disappointed – they didn't get the hug on the platform that they had been hoping for.

My mother was taken to a hotel in the centre of the city, and that's where I was taken too. There, at last, in a function room, our eyes were finally able to meet. My mother wept as she came over to me and took both my cheeks in her hands. She closed her eyes, while I kept mine open, unable to say a word. *Luda, Luda*, she said, *too much time has passed . . .* She had expected to find her little girl, and instead she found a woman. I was still me, but I had changed a lot.

In fact, I didn't have the opportunity to talk to her. All the journalists had run to the hotel, where they were brought into the function room. Also present in the room were the highest authorities of the Soviet Union. They wanted their share of the glory – and also their share of the photo opportunity. The hours passed frantically. After the hug, I had to go to the Kremlin. I looked at my mother Anna and realized that this wasn't the moment of confrontation I had feared. Mama Bronisława followed us like a shadow. Her presence in itself said a lot: I was still hers.

The Soviet authorities decided to take me to the most beautiful places in the Soviet Union, the homeland that would have been mine if I hadn't been deported to Poland. Their plan was to make me stay there, but they didn't know that the marriage orchestrated by Mama Bronisława was a big obstacle in their path.

Over the days that followed, it wasn't possible for me to meet my mother Anna on my own. From Moscow I was taken to Leningrad. Then, by plane, to Crimea, to the Caucasus, all with various journalists in our wake. The country's most important newspapers put me on the front page. They talked about me on the radio and on television. I was making news.

The authorities had arranged a future for me without my knowledge. They asked me to stay in their country and enrol at university. Wherever I wanted to live and study, they would make it possible. There were no obstacles, no economic problems: they would pay for it all. Mama Anna followed me step by step, waiting for the right moment to be able to talk to me. I took my time; I didn't reply to the suggestions of the authorities. I held back and was evasive.

Finally, after a few days, they took me by train to my mother's house. Here again there were big celebrations. The whole city was in the streets; everyone wanted to see me. There was a great crowd and banners to welcome me at the station. At her house, I met her family. I had twin sisters I didn't know about, born in 1947. Relatives had wanted to call one of them Lyudmila. My mother Anna had resisted that with all her might. She felt that I was still alive. She wouldn't have allowed one of her daughters to have the same name as me.

It was here that we finally talked. I held back nothing of what I had inside. I told her I was quite angry. I asked her why she hadn't come looking for me, how it was possible that in all those years it hadn't occurred to her to try and come to Poland. She had left me there – how come she had never thought about the possibility that I might still be alive in the same place?

Mama Anna wept and at the same time she smiled warmly at me. And she asked me to let her explain. She said that in the Soviet Union they had told her over and over again from the very start that all the Belarussian and Russian children that had been saved in the German and Polish camps had been taken back to the Soviet Union and put in the country's orphanages. They led her to believe that if I was still alive, she should look for me there and nowhere else. They told her that when the Red Army liberated the camps they brought home all our compatriots. She told me she looked all over the Soviet Union asking everyone for information. That she travelled as much as she could, knocking on the door of all the orphanages. She told me she mentioned the number of the tattoo on my arm in all the places to which deportees had been sent, but that she hadn't found a trace of me. It was as if I had disappeared; she didn't know what to do. The authorities didn't allow her to travel to Poland, or else she would have left in spite of everything, hoping that I might be alive even if I hadn't managed to get back to the Soviet Union.

And she added that she thought about me every single day. Every time my birthday came round she would bake a cake, open a bottle of champagne and celebrate with tears in her eyes. The twins asked: *Mama, whose birthday is it?*

Your sister's, she would say. *And one day I'm sure you will meet her.*

And they looked her in the eye, not understanding at first. Then, as they grew up, they did understand and thought that all trace of me had disappeared for ever.

She repeated that she really thought I was alive. That she had believed it for all these years.

I listened to her, and believed her. My heart believed her. I looked at my sisters and realized that there was no connection between us. They had grown up without me; they were part of my family, but it felt as if theirs was a different one. I noticed that with the passing hours they became increasingly impatient. Mama Anna was alone with me, and they were worried that she would forget about them. And it wasn't easy for me to relate to them. They were a bit jealous of me, and probably I was of them too.

I stayed in Russia for a few weeks in all. After that initial

150

meeting with my mother, there were also others. I told her about myself, about my adoptive parents, about my life in Oświęcim after the liberation of the camp.

Day after day, the moment of truth approached. Mama Anna was convinced that I would stay in the Soviet Union. She couldn't consider any other possibilities. She said as much straight out to Mama Bronisława. She said: *I didn't put Luda on your doorstep. I didn't ask you to take her with you. It was the war that did it all.*

And Mama Bronisława replied: *What was I supposed to do? Leave her in that barrack to die of cold and hunger? She would have ended up in an orphanage. Who knows what might have happened to her! Instead I looked after her, I saved her. If she's here now, it's partly down to me.*

I left Birkenau camp like a skeleton, in very poor health. I had a thousand problems: I had tuberculosis, I was anaemic, my body was covered with pustules; I was an insecure child, agitated, defenceless. Everyday objects were a novelty to me, things I had never seen before. Wherever I went I assumed that rats and dogs were going to appear at any moment, that Dr Mengele was about to resurface from nowhere and take me away. Mama

Bronisława had really taken me from rock bottom, protected me and brought me up.

How could I deny all that?

How could I not be grateful?

During the days I spent travelling in the Soviet Union I came to a realization: I couldn't disown Mama Anna, the efforts she had made to keep me alive in Birkenau, her love when she deprived herself of food to give it to me, her concern that I should never forget who I was and that I should not forget her. But two mothers had been part of my life, two mothers whom, if I looked deep inside myself, I loved in the same way and with the same intensity.

To be honest, I couldn't have lived without Mama Bronisława, without the meadows of Oświęcim, its residents, my friends. And yet it would have been impossible for me to detach myself entirely from Mama Anna, now that I had finally found her again. I couldn't say to her: *I'm sorry, I'm off. I have a different mother now and it's not you.* I couldn't say that, and didn't want to.

When I went back to the hotel in Moscow that the Soviet authorities had booked for me, I felt torn. Because I understood very clearly that Anna wanted me entirely to herself, and at the same time that Bronisława would never let that happen. My natural and adoptive fathers kept themselves out of the spotlight. They loved me, certainly, but more discreetly. That's how it was throughout all those years at any rate. Their presence was important to me, however, even if it was quieter and more withdrawn.

The journalists, and a whole country with them, observed me and I think partly guessed my state of mind. For the first time in my life I wondered whether I too, tough Lidia who was afraid of nothing after Birkenau, would capitulate and admit that I didn't know what to do. Whether I too might not weep and say to them: *You do it; I can't choose*. Being with Mama Anna or Mama Bronisława was too big a decision for me.

The present without a past is a very thin layer. It crumbles in a moment and nothing remains but rubble. I couldn't go back to Poland while denying my past, and at the same time I couldn't remain in Russia while repudiating all the years I had spent in my adoptive family.

On display in the corridors of the hotel were some photographs from the war. One showed a cocky-looking Adolf Hitler, perhaps announcing that soon all of Russia, Leningrad included, would capitulate. How wrong his certainties proved to be.

As I looked at that photograph something changed within me, and suddenly I had a sense of what I should do.

I knew I wouldn't defeat this challenge by being certain.

I wouldn't beat it by trying to be something that I wasn't. On the contrary, I had to yield to my emotions; I had to allow them to guide me and act on that basis.

In a flash I understood that the little girl in the camp, the one who had been denied everything, learned one thing very well: to accept the circumstances that life puts in front of us. Now I also understood that there was only one thing that I could and had to do: accept the circumstances as they were. Two mothers were fighting over me, competing for me. I had to accept that situation, which meant saying to them: *I'm not choosing Bronisława or Anna because I have two mothers. I choose both.* I would go back to live in Poland because I was married to a Polish man and because that was where I had grown up, as long as Mama Anna could come and see me every now and again and I could go and see her in Russia.

Don't cry because the enemy will hear you, Mama Anna said to me in the camp. It was an important lesson, which I had often put into practice in the course of my life. That ability to resist in difficult situations, to be like a chameleon and change colour according to the circumstances, had also come to the fore during my first days in the Soviet Union. I reflected and understood that I could also adapt to this new situation: to live with two mothers and at the same time persuade them that this was the right way forward for them. In making my decision I was strengthened by love, the affection that I felt for both of them in spite of everything. I was really making the best choice for them as well.

Bronisława and Anna were speechless. I'd made the decision on my own without communicating it to either of them. The media were pressing, asking where I planned to go and live. They took it for granted that I would stay in the Soviet Union. I wasn't moving anywhere, I replied. The child from the camp who had found her mother was going back to Poland.

After their initial surprise, Bronisława and Anna understood. Anna was less happy, of course. She cried and didn't know what to say. She thought it was her fault. She thought that if she'd done more to find me just after the liberation of Birkenau, many things would have changed. But to tell the truth, she hadn't witnessed the liberation. She was marching towards death along with other Jews and deportees shortly before the arrival of the Red Army. She was only told about the liberation subsequently. Even though she felt I was alive, she didn't know for certain.

At any rate, she calmed down. And with unexpected generosity she told me she accepted my decision. That if my happiness depended on it, this was the right solution. She also hugged Bronisława, thanking her for what she had done and for what she would do. And she made me promise that we would see each other soon.

So, for me, the hug between them became the best moment of the trip. Obviously my hug with Anna was another, but seeing Anna and Bronisława hugging one another evoked a powerful feeling that dissolved all the accumulated tension.

I went back to Oświęcim with my husband and my adoptive parents. The city welcomed me with a warm summer sun. The water in the river was starting to fill with trout and little fishes. In the fields the primulas had already made way for a scattering of daisies. The grass was growing tall and some farmers had already done the first cutting with their scythes to provide fodder for their animals. The first leaves had appeared on the trees, along with some blossoms. In the evening the old people played cards in the street. Women waved from their windows. There was a zest for life.

I was at peace in my heart. I thought I had made the right decision. The Soviet politicians would allow my mother to travel whenever she wanted. And I would be able to do the same. The restrictions would be relaxed.

The echo of the last days I had spent in the Soviet Union had reached Poland loud and clear. Here too I was welcomed with affection. People came running along the street to say hello to me. They were happy that I had chosen to stay in their country.

I was proud of my decision, and when we got home, Mama Bronisława immediately started doing up the house. She knew that Mama Anna would be coming soon, and she didn't want to lose face.

Before Anna arrived, though, her letters did. Since I left Moscow, she wrote one a day. She would never stop: until the end of her life not a single day passed without her writing a letter. I found one every morning in my letterbox in Poland. Sometimes she just wrote a few words. For example: *My Luda, I love you so much and I miss you, your Mama*. At other times she would tell me at length why she wasn't able to look for me after the camp. She wanted to apologize once again. She said she was wounded by my inability to understand. She wrote to me over and over again that it wasn't her fault.

And from those letters I learned that separation from me had been an agonizing experience, and that it would never leave her. It wasn't just the scars of the violence we had suffered in Birkenau; more than anything, her interrupted relationship with me was a wound that could not be entirely healed, even though we had found one another again. Often, along the edge of her letters she would draw little flowers and hearts, with my name written in them.

I didn't reply every day, but I did write often. I understood that she needed me, and needed my love; she needed reassurance that I loved her too, that I wouldn't forget her and that I had understood that all those years spent far apart had not been her fault. That the blame lay with that terrible, unjust war and the Nazi criminals who tore out the heart of our Europe. Mama Bronisława no longer needed to hide the correspondence from me. The first letters still came to her address. And, in fact, she was often the one who brought them to me. *Your mother has written to you again*, she would say with a smile, holding out the latest missive. She too demonstrated great generosity. She accepted that my heart had been divided in two; she accepted Anna's letters as she accepted her frequent visits to Poland.

The first of these came not long after I went back to my homeland. Anna arrived without my father as they couldn't both afford to come. She was wearing her finest clothes, and obviously wanted to look her best. It was almost twenty years since she had left Birkenau. She hadn't been back since then. She came on the train even though it was a big effort for her, because travelling in a convoy,

158

since the deportation, revived the old traumas. To make matters worse, she was taking a train towards Poland, and towards the camp that had marked her life for ever.

Mama Bronisława welcomed her like a queen. She spoke to her gently, smiling often, and prepared her best food. Even so, she had her sleep at my place: I lived alone with my husband, and had room for my mother. Mama Anna wanted me to tell her what my childhood had been like. She asked me about the games I'd played, and she wanted to see the room where I'd slept during all those years. Lots of people came into the street to greet her. They gave her flowers. Everyone knew our story. She asked me to translate for her. She asked the people to tell her about me; she wanted to know what I had done as a child, how they saw me.

It's true, you can't go back in time. Certain wounds, certain separations, can't be erased. Months and years had passed; there was no way of going back to the beginning. Still, at a certain point in your life there may be an opportunity to redeem what's been. It wasn't pointless; it wasn't just painful for Mama Anna to come here, walk where I had walked, see the places where I had grown up without her. It was a bit like taking back something you weren't able to have. It was a bit like going back in time to rub balm on wounds that were still bleeding.

One day she asked me to go with her to Birkenau. She wanted us to go there on our own. She was nervous, I could tell, but I was aware that she needed this visit. She wanted to act as my guide, tell me what she had seen, remind me what it had been like, so that I would fully understand what she had done for me.

We approached the camp on a hot and sunny morning. It's only a few kilometres from Oświęcim. But Mama Anna couldn't climb over the gate, so she couldn't get in. She felt ill and looked as if she was about to faint. It was too emotional an experience. I had to call a doctor to help her feel better.

The second time was better. Anna managed to keep her feelings under control. She stopped for a moment outside the gate. She needed to catch her breath. As far as she was concerned the Germans were still in there, the dogs still barking. *It wasn't like this*, she suddenly said to me in a low voice. *You remember? It was very cold. It was dark and the wind lashed our frightened faces. It was a cold that spoke to us and said: this is the house of death. Now everything is filled with light, but that's not how it was.*

I know, I replied, and didn't say anything else.

The gate was open. We were the only ones to pass through it, and there was no one else around. A door was open under the big tower on the right. Through it we could see the ladder leading up to the sentry room overlooking all the barracks, the tracks, the ovens at the end of the camp. Anna seemed tempted to climb up, but she opted not to. She walked slowly along the train tracks for the first few yards. She looked around, stopped for a moment again, and wept. She rested her head against my chest. I let her get it all out. Then we walked on to the place where the convoys had stopped.

This, she said, *is the place where we got out with your grandparents. They dragged us violently out. Old people fell to the ground – pregnant women, men and children, all together. They immediately separated us from your grandparents. There was nothing I could do to save them. I was holding you in my arms. I looked for them at least to say goodbye to them one last time, but it wasn't possible. I remember so much resignation. None of the people who got out of the trucks dared to rebel. I obeyed the orders in silence. It was too cold, and any kind of thought was dulled. Like those who came after us, we'd just been on an inhuman journey. No one could even imagine making any kind of rebellious gesture.*

She bent down and stroked the stones on the ground. The ash from the ovens had settled on them over months. The earth itself was made of the remains of our loved ones, hundreds of thousands of innocents dispatched to their deaths. The earth was the flesh of our flesh.

We approached the barrack in which she had been kept. *I remember the first time they brought me here*, she told me. *It was the very worst moment of my imprisonment because they separated me from you. It was inconceivable for me to be without you. You were so young, so defenceless. I was holding you tightly in my arms when they took you away. Would you survive? I had no idea. I was terrified for you, for your life. Luckily I found other Belarussian women in the barrack. We were among the youngest and fittest. That was why they assigned us to work on the river just outside the camp. That was a stroke of luck for me. It was how I sometimes managed to get hold of onions and bring them to you. When I came to give you some food and found that you were still alive my heart burst with joy. I was still afraid, of course I was, but seeing you able to survive, seeing that you had already grown up a bit helped me a lot.*

I let her go inside the barrack on her own. She came out after a few minutes, in tears. *It's empty*, was all she said, and attempted a smile.

We walked towards the space where the ovens had stood. They were gone now.

You remember the smoke? she asked me. *It rose high, sometimes red and at other times black. The smell of burning flesh was unbearable.*

Beside the ovens there was still, dug into the ground,

162

a gas chamber. It had lost its roof, and you could see its internal structure from above.

They gassed so many, she said. *They put them in there and pushed them around. Sometimes when we went to the river we passed very close by the lines of people who were about to die. They were all aware that going in there meant never coming out. When the showers came on the luckiest were the ones standing underneath one. They died more quickly and suffered less. The others took longer to go; they died on their feet, their bodies crammed among the others.*

Near the ovens some people had left little stones. We touched them with our hands. They were the stones that some deportees who had returned to the camp had decided to put there in memory of their loved ones. My mother set one down too, in memory of my grandparents and all those who didn't survive. Then we made our way towards some far-off barracks placed on the left of the tracks as you entered the camp. During her detention my mother wasn't able to go into that part of the camp. Now she wanted to walk down every path, go into every barrack to see. In my barrack she touched the drawings on the walls with her hands. She caressed the wooden boards where I and the others had slept. She wanted to see the latrines, the kitchens. She wept as she hugged me.

We left by a door a hundred yards from the main

entrance. She couldn't believe that we could leave unhindered. When she spotted the gate she quickened her pace; she was in a hurry to leave. It was as if the darkness was attacking her again. As if she was afraid that the past might come back. Not all survivors managed to see the camps again, revisit those places. She did. Not because she was better than the others. Everyone is different. Anna managed, but once we were back home she looked me in the eyes and said: *Never again. I never want to go there again.*

7

WHAT I'M TELLING HERE, MY STORY, sadly like that of many others, might seem incredible. Or perhaps the product of a sick imagination. And yet it's all true: I'm one of the last remaining witnesses of the Nazi horror. Even though I was only a child when I entered Birkenau, I remember many things. The experiences I had have been imprinted on my memory and influenced the whole of my existence, my childhood, my adolescence and now even my old age.

In spite of everything, in spite of years when I managed to overcome those experiences, they are still deeply rooted within me. It's impossible for me to set aside what happened, or to forget it.

I understand survivors of the Shoah who can't summon the courage to bear witness. The darkness that enveloped them is deep. And it also produces deep feelings of guilt. I have those, every day. Why did I get away when so many other children didn't? Why did thousands die and a few others didn't? Why was it them and not me?

These are questions to which I have no answer. For years I couldn't summon the courage to say anything. Once I had left I went back into the camp to play with my contemporaries, but I said very little about the barrack, about Dr Mengele, about the torture, the months I spent in there and what happened. The faces of my friends who didn't make it will never leave me. I see them lying on the wooden tables, in the corridors, in the kitchens, terrified and trying to find nooks to hide in. I see them in front of me even now, at this moment. It's true: like everyone else in the camp, I fought fiercely to survive. If Mengele came into the barrack, I fought so that others would be taken instead of me. And it was natural to act like that. But what was natural in there became guilt once I was out. That's why I understand the ones who don't talk. That's why I don't judge the ones who can't say anything, who spend their whole lives just trying to forget. For me, on the other hand, talking about it meant freeing yourself from at least some of the weight you carry, and allowing love to spread.

What love? The love I have within me for life, for my loved ones, for all those who are, like myself, on the difficult path of life.

Auschwitz and Birkenau are not a symbol; they are reality. In the time of the camps they were the biggest death factory ever conceived in the world. My tragedy was to find myself at the epicentre of those crimes. Because I was a child I didn't understand why I was there or why I couldn't be with my mother. I very quickly worked out, by instinct I would say, how you needed to behave in order to survive. I understood that I was in the middle of a struggle not to give in: we had to fight with all our strength for a slice of bread or a bit of watery broth, the only food we child deportees were allowed.

Terrible things happened in the camp, things I didn't fully understand at the time but learned later as an adult. The German pharmaceutical industries and the country's scientists performed experiments on women and children, and particularly on twins. Dr Mengele, the Angel of Death, was there. His task was to create human beings with exceptional characteristics that would be useful to the Nazis when it came to populating Europe after its conquest. His name resonated straight away and imprinted itself on my mind. We knew that he was giving children painful injections, that he put painful eyewash in their eyes; now I know that he wanted to obtain a human being with blue irises, the colour of 'Aryan' eyes according to the Nazis. He also tested vaccines on us, on behalf of the German pharmaceutical industry. We were used as guinea pigs and were only kept alive in the camp for that purpose. For Mengele, we were nothing but material for his work.

Many of us died. The ones who made it back to the barrack lay almost lifeless on the boards with a high fever for days. Our bodies were almost transparent from having our blood taken. That didn't stop the kapo from taking us for inspection in the open air every morning. Sometimes we had to stay standing for hours. There was no mercy for us. They didn't see us as people, people like themselves, but only as numbers.

Death was our constant companion. We didn't react when corpses were removed from the barrack. The kapo crossed out their names from the list and ordered that the bodies be thrown onto a cart that set off for the crematorium.

I owe my life to certain favourable circumstances, to chance, to my physical resilience, but you might say that in all this tragedy my greatest good fortune was to have my mother, Anna, at the camp – a very courageous young woman, determined to save me.

Sometimes pregnant women would come to the camp. They had been pregnant when they were taken away from their countries, and in spite of the huge physical effort they had managed to survive the train journey. Once they reached Birkenau, they were made to give birth in our barrack. However, as soon as the child was born, it was immediately killed with an injection of phenol, or drowned in a bucket of water. I very clearly remember the gesture with which the mother brought the child to her breast as soon as it was born. She delighted in that new life, holding the flesh of her flesh in her arms. But after a few minutes the child was torn from her to be killed. There was no room for babies in the camp. There was no room for a new life. I remember the expression on the faces of those women: despair, hopeless anguish.

I didn't feel the need to testify all at once.

When I was young, new ex-prisoners would appear in Oświęcim every day. They would stay somewhere in the city before summoning the courage to set foot in the camp again. They were older than me and came from all over the world to return to the place where they had experienced their greatest terror. They would enter the camp on tiptoe and weep. Often they went with a little group of people. Once they were inside some of them felt a natural need to tell their story, to bear witness. I was much younger than they were, and observed them in respectful silence. No one paid any attention to me. I understood that it was their turn to speak.

At home we had a neighbour, Pani Piatkowska, who was a friend of my adoptive mother. She was the wife of the director of a chemical plant. She was educated; a cultivated woman. She often took me for long walks in the countryside around Oświęcim. She was the one who started telling me about what the war had done to the world, and what the Nazi horror had meant for humanity. Every time anyone mentioned the Nazis, I stuck my fingers in my ears. I even hid the tattoo on my arm for a long time. It was this woman who woke me up: *Don't worry about the little things*, she said, *think big*. And again: *One day it will be your turn to tell your story, so get ready. That tattoo says who you are, what they did to you. You needn't be afraid to show it. On the contrary, you should be proud of it. They branded you because they thought you weren't people, but animals, numbers. Let people see it, show it to them so that everyone knows.*

Those words gradually started burrowing away inside me. The meeting with my natural mother after seventeen years apart meant that many people looked for me, asked after me, wanted to know my story. So I too started talking about the camp, about Birkenau, about the Nazi horror. The first invitations to our cultural centres came in, then to schools. It was during those first meetings that I showed my tattoo, that I learned not to be ashamed of having it.

Along the path of bearing witness I was also helped by my son. Yes, I have a son. He was born after several years of marriage. I started telling him about my life when he was little, so he always knew. He grew up with two grand-mothers, one Polish and the other Russian, who only came to Oświęcim from Donetsk every now and again. He knew my story without having been through it. He didn't ex-perience the pain; he was saved from that. Along with me he buried my two mothers. They passed away some years apart, both peacefully.

Mama Bronisława had a special relationship with him. I remember her telling him about me by the fireside, and

about how she had found me in Birkenau. I was a frightened little scrap. She had seen me sitting on my own, cold
and silent. And she chose me; she brought me home to
her house and taught me to live. Because I knew nothing
of 'normal' life.

But she also told him, and this surprised me, about
the time before she knew me. Things she had never said
to me. She told him how, when the Nazis built Birkenau,
she had tried to approach the camp with other relatives.
The land beside the big entrance gate had belonged to
her and sometimes she wanted to go back and see it.
They didn't really know what was happening in there,
although they guessed that it was a death camp. From
a distance they saw the long lines of prisoners in wooden
clogs and striped uniforms walking to work on the site
of a chemicals plant. And they saw them coming back
carrying on their backs the corpses of the ones who had
been killed. One day Mama Bronisława and a friend
tried to approach the inmates with some bread. An SS
man told them to go away and never try it again: *If you
come near this place again*, he said to them, *you'll end up
in here too.*

Watching my son listening to his grandmother, and
seeing his enthusiasm when I intervened to tell him how
I had found my birth mother, and our meeting in Moscow,

was one of the reasons why I decided to bear witness. I do it partly for him, so that men and women like him are aware of what happened.

But it wasn't just my son and Pani Piatkowska. Other people encouraged me to testify. Chief among them was Karol Wojtyła, John Paul II, the first non-Italian pope of the modern era and a Pole. The first time he came to Poland as a pope was in June 1979, a few months after his election to the throne of St Peter. It was a historic visit. We were governed by Edward Gierek, the head of the Polish Communist Party who had assumed power in 1970 after the tragic events in Gdansk and Gdynia, when his predecessor Wladysław Gomułka ordered troops to fire against striking naval shipyard workers protesting over the cost of living. Gierek asked the shipyard workers to help him, and tried to tell them that he was on their side. He became popular among the majority of us Poles. He made it easier for us to travel for the first time and make contact with the West. He allowed us to dream of the possibility of a different life. But after the first period of improvement the country's economy plunged into a deep abyss. It was while the whole of Poland was falling into that black hole that John Paul II paid us a visit. A pope from a country on the other side of the Iron Curtain returned to a place that was still oppressed by the Communist regime. The people were euphoric. I remember many masses being celebrated in our city, and also in Krakow; the faithful suddenly felt confident enough to display their own faith. But there was a great sense of expectation all over Poland, even among laypeople and non-believers.

The Communist authorities, and especially the Moscow government, hid their real feelings behind silence or apparent indifference. In fact, the Kremlin was fully aware of the 'danger' of this trip. It was no coincidence that rumours circulated even in Oświęcim that the Soviet Union had on several occasions asked the Polish Communist regime for information about this man who had been the surprise election to the Chair of St Peter after the thirty-three days of Albino Luciani.

The Kremlin was trying to understand whether the election of a pope from the east might bring friction to the Vatican's relations with the Socialist bloc. Would the Vatican's Ostpolitik, the opening of the Holy See to Communist regimes with a view to saving as many lives as possible and guaranteeing a certain freedom to Catholic communities, continue along the same lines or not. The chief fear was that John Paul II, who was very familiar with the Communist regime, might abandon the existing Ostpolitik and set off on an openly critical line, strengthened by the support of the international community.

At any rate, after his election the whole of Poland sensed that something might finally change. After the Nazi occupation and the oppression of being part of the Soviet Bloc, it seemed possible that this man might bring the freedom that the whole population so wished for. The Pope's trip lasted nine days in all, and, in fact, marked the beginning of a process that would culminate in the fall of the Berlin Wall in 1989.

I was one of those who came to welcome the Pope in Oświęcim. The Pope visited the camp and spoke in very clear terms: 'I have come to kneel on this Golgotha of the contemporary world,' he said, 'on these graves, largely nameless, like the great tomb of the Unknown Soldier. I kneel before all the stones that succeed one another, all carved with the commemoration of the victims of Birkenau.' And he went on: 'In particular, I stop with all of you, dear participants in this encounter, before the stone with the inscription in the Hebrew tongue. This inscription prompts the memory of the people whose sons and daughters were destined for total extermination. This people has its origins in Abraham, the father of our faith, as Paul of Tarsus put it. This very same people which received from God the commandment "Thou shalt not kill" themselves felt to a very particular degree the meaning of killing. No one can pass by this stone indifferently.'

I, too, was in the camp as he said those words. Along with other survivors of the extermination I was inwardly preparing for a brief private moment with the Pope designed especially for us. I was very agitated. I found myself in the presence of a great spiritual teacher and battling feelings welled up in me. I was still thinking of the many things I didn't do. The fact that I was here and many others were not. I was filled once again with feelings of guilt as I awaited my turn. When I met him, John Paul II put his hand on my head. Then he looked me in the eye for a long time, in silence. His gaze left a deep mark on me and pierced my soul.

It was as if he knew everything about me; he knew every aspect of my grief, of my anxiety. It was as if he said, *Don't worry; go and bear witness to what happened to you.*

At that very moment I felt a strength that wasn't mine being born within me. A light was leading me to leave that place and bear witness. I clearly understood that I had to go on, that I had to bear witness, that it was my turn to come into the open, in spite of all my justified feelings of guilt. I was not to be afraid, ever again. I had to go and tell everyone what the hell of Auschwitz-Birkenau was like, what the Nazi horror had been, what the extermination camps had been like in those dark years. I had to speak. I had to do it for all the people for whom I felt guilty. For my barrack-mates, for their innocent eyes. I had to do it for them, for their memory and for the future of the generations to come. I had to do it for all of us. The survivor Liliana Segre was right when she said that if we forget the past, we will repeat that violence and hate it. And it was true: it was to avoid a repetition of what happened that I had to find the strength and courage to tell my story.

Ten years later there was another momentous event, this time for the world. I was nearly forty-nine when the Berlin Wall came down, in November 1989. I remember that in Poland the anti-Soviet Solidarność movement had won the elections a few weeks before. The victory came as a huge shock to everybody. Solidarność won more or less all the seats where it stood. As early as August, in fact, it was clear the prime minister was there. There was euphoria in the streets. Soon the Eastern Bloc would be no more and we would all be free. I remember the pictures on television of the Berlin Wall coming down; I remember my feelings and those of my loved ones. I clearly remember that my thoughts turned immediately to my mother: now she would be able to reach me without any particular problems. I don't have a very close relationship with my sisters. There are too many years and too many miles between us. It was very different with my mother. After that day she was able to come to Poland more often, and also stayed with me for a long time.

My two mothers are no longer alive, but they both lived on in the stories that I was asked to tell as I travelled around the world. I always finished all my testimonies, especially those in front of an audience of young people, with these words: *The future of the world lies in your hands; what it's like depends on you. It will be up to you alone to ensure that no such abomination ever happens again. It's true, you've never seen Auschwitz in person, but you can know from my words and those of many other witnesses who came before me.*

At first young people struggle to believe what happened to me. They can't believe it. How could one human being have treated another in that way? And yet that's how it was. That's why, today, it is my obligation to tell the story. That beast is stirring again: nationalism, acts of war and hatred between nations, not least religious hatred. They are incredible situations that we thought we had abandoned. How is it possible that even today we no longer listen to one another? Clearly there are people who don't remember the past. But we survivors do not forget. We saw the fall of humanity and we do not want it to be repeated.

I have said it many times and I say it again: my life is made of shadows, but also of light. Among the lights, without a doubt, are the many testimonies that I have taken around the world. On those occasions I also speak of my natural mother, of our relationship, our story. She too saw lights and shadows in her light. Our reunion was not the only light.

Telling the story keeps me alive. It shows me that there is a reason why I didn't die as a little girl – that something, perhaps something on high, wanted it to be like this.

Wojtyła had witnessed the tragedy of the camps at close quarters. He was the one who said that the crime of the Shoah remained an indelible stain in the history of the century that was now drawing to a close. And he would write in the run-up to the 2000 Jubilee *We Remember: A Reflection on the Shoah*, a Vatican document on the Church's responsibility in the Holocaust. He didn't merely condemn the camps and the Nazi horror, but went on to ask forgiveness for the faults of the Church, exhorting believers to purify their own hearts, through repentance for their errors and the lapses of the past. This Pope urged everyone to place themselves humbly before God and examine their own responsibility for the evils of their time.

These were words that struck me. They allowed me to understand for the first time that anti-Jewish prejudices had been present even in the minds and hearts of some Christians, fed, as Wojtyła wrote, by an erroneous interpretation of the New Testament. Unfortunately the anti-Semitism of Christian Europe facilitated the extermination ordered by Hitler. It was for this that the Church asked to be forgiven. For that courage I felt, and continue to feel, close to him.

And, along with him, to Pope Francis.

Francis, too, used similar words when he remembered the Nazi extermination. In the preface to *Extracts from the Torah/Pentateuch with Commentaries from Jews and Christians*, he said he was aware that we had nineteen centuries of Christian anti-Jewish feeling behind us, and that a few decades of dialogue were not much in comparison. Still, he went on, in recent times many things had changed and others were still in the process of changing. We needed to work more intensely to ask forgiveness and repair the damage caused by an incomprehension.

But what struck me more than Francis's words was the silence that he decided to keep during his visit to

Auschwitz extermination camp in 2016. There, in 2006, Benedict XVI wondered: *Where was God in those days? Why, Lord, were you silent? Why were you able to bear all this?* Words that Francis repeated, but only once he had left the camp. His visit was conducted entirely in silence. He passed through the entrance on his own, on foot, head bowed. Then, once he was inside, he got into his electric vehicle to move from one zone of the structure to the other. Then he sat down, still alone and still in silence, on a bench in front of the dormitories where the inmates were locked up, and sat there for over a quarter of an hour, absorbed in deep reflection, sometimes with eyes closed, and hands folded in his lap. Before he continued on his path he approached the gallows from which prisoners were hanged, and kissed one of its posts.

Then he stepped inside the adjacent Block 11, site of the killing of the Franciscan priest Maximilian Kolbe, who volunteered to die instead of a father who had been chosen as one of those sentenced to death by starvation in reprisal for a prisoner escape. Francis went alone into his cell, where the graffiti written on the walls by the inmates is still visible, and sat down in prayer for several minutes. It was that silence that struck me, a silence full of respect for those who lost their lives in there, but also for those who survived but who still bear the indelible marks on their souls.

If on the one hand there is a duty to bear witness, on the other I understand why one might approach this place of death and stay silent. At that precise moment it is hard to find words; even though explanations must be given, it is also possible to show pity without speaking.

It was a warm morning in late May 2021 when I took part in the Wednesday General Audience in the San Damaso Courtyard in the Vatican. It was held there because Covid-19 measures meant that only a limited number of people were allowed inside. The Courtyard welcomed me in fine Renaissance style. I was seated in one of the front rows, and knew that at the end I would have the opportunity for a quick greeting with the Pope. I didn't expect anything in particular, and thought of the first time I saw John Paul II in Poland, about his silence, and I was convinced that this time would be more or less the same.

Francis delivered a brief catechesis on the subject of prayer. It seemed to me that his words were appropriate to what I had seen in the camp: there was a radical objection to prayer, he said, based on something we had all observed. We pray, we ask for things, and yet, sometimes our prayers seem to go unheard. The same was true in Birkenau, I think. How many prayers of the inmates went unheard! The things we requested for ourselves or others, the Pope continued, did not come about. And he went on: we have that experience, often. Then, if the reason that we were praying was noble (like intercession for the healing of a sick person, or for a war to come to an end), this lack of response strikes us as scandalous. Francis wonders: If God is the Father, why does he not listen to us? He who made promises to his children – why does he not answer our pleas? We have all prayed: for the healing of the sickness of a friend, a father, a mother who then passed away: God did not listen to us.

I heard the Pope's words and reflected on how true they were. Often God does not answer our pleas. In my mind I was still there, thinking of the pain of millions of human beings killed in the camps. Many of them were people of faith; they prayed to God and were not heard. And I was glad that Francis did not give answers: the silence of God, whether we liked it or not, remained.

The audience continued, and the Pope's words were read in other languages. Then came the moment of the final greetings. Francis moved towards the people in the front rows. He began to greet them one at a time. He stopped with some of them for several minutes. Eventually he arrived in front of me. I looked at him but didn't know what to say because I don't speak Italian. The person next to me introduced me and briefly told him my story. What could I say? What could I tell him? The words of Pani Piatkowska occurred to me: *Don't be ashamed of your tattoo; it's testimony to who you are; it speaks for you.* I was wearing a blue blouse with white polka dots that also covered my arms. Almost instinctively I decided to roll up the sleeve and uncover my left arm. In short, I showed Francis my tattoo, the 70072 that sums up the whole of my life.

It was at that moment that the Pope spontaneously performed a gesture that I will never be able to forget. He bent down and kissed me on that number, the horror of which I still remember daily even after seventy-seven years. Not a word, as before in his visit to Auschwitz, but an unpremeditated, instinctive, affectionate gesture, which I returned with a hug. And then burst into tears.

I would have to say: the Pope's kiss strengthened me and reconciled me even more with the world. Francis and I understood one another with our eyes; we didn't have to say anything; there was no need to speak. That number, the number with which I was marked as a little girl when

I had just arrived at the camp, the number that my mother repeated for years in an attempt to find me again, was blessed with a kiss from the Pope. Evil can turn to good, a light for all people. The number that speaks of a terrible reality can become a light for others – that is the message of the Pope's kiss.

It may seem strange, but I don't know how to hate. I know, in fact, that if I hate, I will suffer even more, certainly more than many who contributed to my terrible fate. If I was saved, I owe it in part to an extraordinary force that watched over me from above. I am devoutly convinced of it. But if I survived, if that force allowed me to escape alive, it was not to exchange hatred for hatred but to testify to what evil was like, and the fact that good can always prevail.

For months I was trapped inside an unthinkable reality. For this testimony, so that people may know that the impossible can become flesh, that it can become real. My attempt to bear witness not only to what happened, but also to the peace that can emerge victorious in spite of everything and assert itself. It is for goodness, for that peace finally granted me after the camp, that I tell my story, that I speak. If I were not a bringer of peace, I would not be performing my task.

I lived through the longest period spent by any child in the camp. Many of my companions did not make it out alive. I did. My mission is therefore to speak for those who did not survive and tell everyone that they must take care lest the darkness return, so that mothers need not weep for their own children, so that everyone is spared having to lose their own parents and their own loved ones.

I have listened several times to the testimony of Liliana Segre. I identify with her when she talks of the commandant of that last camp, a person whose name she does not know. She says he was a cruel SS man, harsh and inflexible, exactly as his beliefs had told him to be. Exactly like many that I met, too. She says that before fleeing Birkenau, when the Russians were about to arrive, like all German soldiers he threw away his weapons and abandoned his uniform so that he could go home and maintain that he had had nothing to do with war crimes. Segre explains that she had fed on hatred and vengeance. She had lost everything, she was a witness to unimaginable acts of violence, of hatred and absolute evil, and she had dreamed of achieving her revenge. When she saw that SS man's pistol at her feet she thought she had reached the final moment, when she would pick up that weapon and shoot him. It seemed like the right ending to the story. It was, she says, a huge and powerful temptation, and it lasted for a moment. But then something happened that I understand very well: she was not like her murderer. She had chosen life and could not have killed anyone for any reason. She did not pick up the pistol and she became the free, peace-loving woman that she is today. I feel close to her because, like her, I decided not to cultivate hatred and vengeance, but to stay myself, a woman who wanted only to love.

Those days almost eighty years ago are very far away. That autumn of 1943, the transport to Birkenau on cattle trucks and then imprisonment. I have never learned to hate, and even today I don't know how to do it. Those who hate suffer much more than those who are hated. Because often those who are hated don't know it. But those who hate know that they are hating and hatred can only lead to death, to personal and collective destruction.

Hatred is a feeling that destroys, and that's it. It doesn't create anything, while the world needs creation and not destruction. In the history of the world there are many good figures who worked for that: I'm thinking of Jesus, Buddha, Gandhi, Martin Luther King, Mother Teresa of

Calcutta. They are people who have given much to humanity and received practically nothing in return.

Hatred destroys.

My task is to love and testify to the light which, in spite of the darkness, enwraps us and doesn't abandon us.

Acknowledgements

This book was born on 26 May 2021 when, to everyone's surprise, at the end of the Wednesday General Audience, Pope Francis met Lidia Maksymowicz and wanted to kiss the number tattooed on her arm by the Nazis when she arrived with her young mother at Birkenau camp in 1943. So my thanks go first of all to Francis, who was kind enough to give this work a brief introduction.

Obviously my special thanks to Lidia, who agreed to tell her story for the first time. And to Anna, who patiently translated our long discussions, and to Renata, who helped me to engage in dialogue with Lidia both in Krakow and in Castellamonte near Turin.

Lidia owed her participation in the Audience to the association 'La Memoria Viva'. The association, which has dealt for some time with the recovery of historical memory with an approach open to new themes and reflections, made a beautiful documentary dedicated to Lidia: *77072 The Little Girl Who Couldn't Hate*. It was that film that inspired this book. I therefore thank the whole association, among others Elso, Felicia and in particular Roberto Falletti, its president, because without his and their help this book would not have been possible.

Particular thanks to Jadwiga Pinderska Lech, President of the Foundation for the Victims of Auschwitz-Birkenau. It was she, as head of the publishing house of the State Museum of Auschwitz-Birkenau, who gave voice to the survivors. Without her, without her patient reading of our drafts, this book could not have seen the light of day.

Many thanks also to Professor Ugo Rufino, director of the Italian Cultural Institute in Krakow, for his valuable interest.

My last words of thanks are for those who have been closest to me during these months, particularly my family and my agent Vicki Satlow, who believed in this story from the first moment, and Michela di Solferino, who helped me to improve the text.

Thanks to all

Paolo Rodari